Praise

M000086427

Facilitating Dialogue

"*Facilitating Dialogue* is an essential body of work that contributes to the professional dialogue for all those involved in both ensuring stability and restoring peace. Most important, it frames potential solutions with real examples and creates a better understanding of the challenges with these undertakings. High praise to USIP once again! Well done!"

—**Edward C. Cardon,** Major General, United States Army

"An engrossing collection of cases of track II dialogue processes in five regions, this volume should find a place on the shelf of educators and train-ers and in the luggage of practitioners. Seven well-structured and accessible case essays provide essential background to the narratives. Most important, the collection is rich in lessons to be drawn from the cases and an impor-tant addition to the case literature on nonofficial diplomacy."

—**Chester A. Crocker,** James R. Schlesinger Professor of Strategic Studies, Edmund A. Walsh School of Foreign Service, Georgetown University

"The U.S. Institute of Peace has pioneered the facilitated dialogue as a technique for conflict prevention and resolution. David Smock and Dan Serwer have assembled accounts of seven such USIP-led efforts. These all involve peacebuilding at the retail level, engaging individuals, albeit influ-ential ones, not governments. Personalities naturally play a major role, and these accounts are full of touching, inspirational, sometimes amusing, and often frustrating moments. Building peace from the bottom up is no sub-stitute for traditional diplomacy, but as this volume illustrates, it is often an essential support and even prerequisite for government-led efforts."

—**James Dobbins,** director of the International Security and Defense Policy Center and the RAND Corporation and former U.S. assistant secretary of state.

"Testimony to the vital work the U.S. Institute of Peace does in the field, as well as an important contribution to theories and strategies of conflict resolution and the track 1.5 dialogue approach in particular."

—**Bruce W. Jentleson,** Duke University

"With daily reports of the horrifying humanitarian consequences of violent conflicts around the world, *Facilitating Dialogue* offers fascinating practical and realistic alternatives to seeking peace and justice through dialogue among conflicting parties. The insights on how to build problem-solving relationships before, during, and after conflicts drawn from specific case studies are refreshingly honest, down-to-earth, and thought-provoking both for veterans and newcomers to peacebuilding processes."

—**Søren Jessen-Petersen,** professor, SAIS, Johns Hopkins University, and former Special Representative of the UN Secretary-General, Kosovo.

"Smock and Serwer have pulled together a set of rich case studies that reinforce the takeaway that facilitated dialogue and track II diplomacy are a crucial, if underappreciated, tool in enhancing communication and helping to define shared interests. In a number of the case studies, increasing the parties' understanding of each others' grievances is a critical outcome and arguably a prerequisite to progress in any track I negotiation. The depth and diversity of these cases demonstrates the value of USIP's work and, more broadly, the need for an expansion of track II and facilitated dialogue efforts at peacebuilding globally."

—**John Prendergast,** cofounder, Enough Project and former USIP executive fellow

"This book makes a fundamental point: Resolution of deep-rooted conflict requires more than the traditional instruments of conflict resolution such as mediation, negotiation, and arbitration. It requires a comprehensive and intensive political process aimed not just at resolving issues but at transforming the conflictual relationships that fuel those issues. The practitioners featured here exemplify the careful analysis of the interactions among parties to conflict and the persistence in gradually developing the relationships that can grow out of wisely constructed dialogue sustained over time."

—**Harold H. Saunders,** president of the International Institute for Sustained Dialogue, former member of the National Security Council staff and assistant secretary of state.

Facilitating Dialogue

Facilitating Dialogue

USIP'S WORK IN
CONFLICT ZONES

David R. Smock and Daniel Serwer
editors

UNITED STATES INSTITUTE OF PEACE PRESS
Washington, D.C.

The views expressed in this book are those of the authors alone. They do not necessarily reflect views of the United States Institute of Peace.

UNITED STATES INSTITUTE OF PEACE
2301 Constitution Avenue, NW
Washington, DC 20037
www.usip.org

First published 2012

To request permission to photocopy or reprint materials for course use, contact the Copyright Clearance Center at www.copyright.com. For print, electronic media, and all other subsidiary rights e-mail permissions@usip.org

Printed in the United States of America

The paper used in this publication meets the minimum requirements of American National Standards for Information Science—Permanence of Paper for Printed Library Materials, ANSI Z39.48-1984.

Library of Congress Cataloging-in-Publication Data

Facilitating dialogue : USIP's work in conflict zones / David R. Smock and Daniel Serwer, editors.
     p. cm.
  Includes index.
  ISBN 978-1-60127-140-2 (alk. paper)
  1. United States Institute of Peace—History. I. Smock, David R.
II. Serwer, Daniel, Ph.D.
  JZ5524.U55F33 2012
  327.1'720973—dc23

                                              2012017403

Contents

Introduction

David R. Smock

International peacebuilding is a complex and fraught process, one in which efforts fail more often than they succeed, although failures can of course plant the seeds for later success. Successful peacebuilding takes several forms and can occur at several levels of society.

This volume focuses on one form at one level in six countries using eight case studies. The form is facilitated dialogue, which is neatly framed in the context of Track 1 and Track 2 diplomacy.

Track 1 diplomacy is conducted directly between official representatives of the state, although third-party negotiators can be involved. Track 2 diplomacy is also international and direct but is unofficial in that participants do not have the authority to make binding agreements, though they do typically have access to government decision-makers. Facilitated dialogue, unlike Track 1 and Track 2 diplomacy, can apply to domestic as well as to international affairs. It is a technique—typically but not always unofficial, usually informal, and always third party.[1]

The case studies in this volume focus on the middle level of society in Colombia, Iraq, Israel-Palestine, Kosovo, Nigeria, and Nepal. By analyzing each case in some detail and then drawing comparative conclusions, this volume helps illuminate how facilitated dialogue can successfully be undertaken to resolve both international conflicts and domestic conflict in foreign countries.

What exactly, then, is facilitated dialogue? It has been neatly described as "a conversation using a neutral third person, not invested in either the relationships or the substance of the conflict, to assist the parties in over-

---

1. See Ronald J. Fisher, ed., *Paving the Way: Contributions of Interactive Conflict Resolution to Peace-making* (Lanham, MD: Lexington Books, 2005).

coming their barriers to effective communication."[2] It includes three core components. The first is "being sensitive to when interactions cease to be productive and intervening to promote a return to effective dialogue or moving to another, more easily manageable topic." Second is "structuring the discussion of issues in terms of underlying interests." Third is "organizing topics to achieve early consensus on less-difficult ones, thus giving the participants a sense of accomplishment and progress."[3] All forms of facilitated dialogue value inclusivity, respectfulness, transparency, openness, and authenticity.

Diana Chigas has described the generic goals of unofficial peacemaking processes generally as "[attempting] to provide an environment that is low-key, non-judgmental, non-coercive, and safe, and to create a process in which participants feel free to share perceptions, fears and needs, and to explore ideas for resolution, free of the constraints of government positions." They are, she continues, "designed to encourage the development of mutual understanding of differing perceptions and needs, the creation of new ideas, and strong problem-solving relationships."[4] They are particularly well suited to addressing conflicts that are not primarily over resource allocation but instead based on identity differences and conflicts in which the transformation of relationships is critical.

Relationships, as John Paul Lederach emphasizes, are both the source of conflict and the basis for long-term resolution of that conflict.[5] Reconciliation is central to the peacebuilding process. It "involves the creation of the social space where both truth and forgiveness are validated and joined together, rather than being forces in an encounter in which one must win out over the other."[6] It seeks to create an encounter where the participants focus on their relationships with the goal of creating new perceptions and a shared experience.[7] It reframes the conflict to enable the participants to "embrace the painful past and the necessary shared future as a means of dealing with the present."[8]

---

2. Michael Landrum, AMERICORD, http://www.mediate.com/landrumdobbins/p.42.cfm (website no longer active).

3. Ibid.

4. Diana Chigas, "Track II (Citizen) Diplomacy," *Beyond Intractability*, August 2003, http://www.beyondintractability.org/bi-essay/track2-diplomacy.

5. John Paul Lederach, *Building Peace: Sustainable Reconciliation in Divided Societies* (Washington, DC: U.S. Institute of Peace, 1997), 26.

6. Ibid., 29.

7. Ibid., 30.

8. Ibid., 35.

Lederach has also been helpful in pointing out the value of focusing on middle-range leadership. These men and women usually have access to top decision-makers but are not as constrained as their superiors by political and other pressures. Hence they have greater flexibility of action, new thinking, and movement.

An instructive example is the Inter-Tajik Dialogue, a Track 2 diplomatic effort. Harold Saunders explained its goal as being "to engage representative citizens from the conflicting parties in designing steps to be taken in the political arena to change perceptions and stereotypes, to create a sense that peace might to possible, and to involve more and more of their compatriots."[9] As in other comparable processes, the participants are influential members of the parties who engage in direct but private interaction. The facilitators are knowledgeable, impartial, and skilled scholar-practitioners.

Although it is often difficult to measure their precise impact on resolving deep-seated conflict, unofficial processes can contribute to ripening a conflict for resolution or management. They can clarify misinformation about the other side and allow for comprehension of the suffering by the other side. "The development of an empathetic understanding of the experiences, perspectives, and needs of the other side forms an initial basis for trust."[10] This in turn helps stimulate an ongoing relationship. Improved communication between the opposing sides is often a positive outcome as well.

Facilitated dialogue and Track 2 diplomacy can provide opportunities for moderate voices to be developed, reinforced, and heard in the wider society. The voices most often heard in zones of intense conflict are those at the extremes. The moderates tend to be marginalized or forced into exile. Facilitated dialogue and Track 2 diplomacy can give them a platform, both for their voices to be heard and to help them form coalitions across conflict lines.[11]

Two other practitioners of Track 2 diplomacy and facilitated dialogue, John Davies and Edward Kaufman, underscore the informal approach. "Unofficial, facilitated face-to-face dialogue, free of institutional policy constraints," they write, "can allow communication, understanding, rehumanization of the enemy, relationship building and reframing of the conflict as a

---

9. Harold Saunders and Randa Slim, *The Inter-Tajik Dialogue: From Civil War Towards Civil Society* (London: Conciliation Resources, 1993), http://www.c-r.org/our-work/accord/tajikistan/inter-tajik-dialogue.php.

10. Chigas, 5.

11. Ibid., 6.

shared problem to be solved rather than a battle to be won or lost."[12] Relationships between people, they say, are critical. They go on to point out the importance of expertise on the part of the facilitators. "Facilitators evaluate or recruit credible representatives of the parties, formulate and get consensus on the ground rules, create a climate of constructive dialogue, ensure that participants do not turn prematurely to negotiation and bargaining, bring the participants to see each other's grievances, and assess interactively what is at issue, separating nonnegotiable needs from negotiable interests."[13]

Several of the studies in this volume tell stories of successful peacebuilding, others describe peacebuilding still in progress, and one did not achieve its principal goals.

The Case Studies

Chapter 1 presents the first case study, the Triangle of Death in Iraq in 2007. Mahmoudiya, a rural district of 400,000 people approximately twenty miles from the center of Baghdad, and home to more than fifty clans, became the locus of bloody sectarian and interclan strife, a haven for terrorists launching attacks in Baghdad. In the early months of 2007, U.S. and Iraqi forces had managed to drive back al-Qaeda and the various militias and armed gangs. Local tribal and government leaders approached the 10th Mountain Division's combat team seeking support for a peace initiative.

Working with Iraqi facilitators and other Iraqi partners, USIP reached out to a wide network of local sheikhs to encourage their participation in a peace process. After several months of such cultivation, preparations were made for a three-day conference. The aim was to encourage the sheikhs to focus on solving current problems rather than on past grievances, to foster a collaborative environment in which they could begin to rebuild trust, and to enable the sheikhs to take collective responsibility for stabilizing and rebuilding their communities.

Complications and challenges were inevitable, and included the murder of two of the invited sheikhs. In the end, however, an agreement was reached and signed by all thirty-two senior tribal leaders. Mahmoudiya has remained relatively peaceful.

---

12. "An Overview," in *Second Track/Citizens Diplomacy*, edited by John Davies and Edward Kaufman (Lanham, MD: Rowman & Littlefield, 2002), 5.
13. Ibid., 27.

Chapter 2 presents the second case, which proved less successful. The goal was to coordinate the reconstruction efforts for refugees in the Diyala province of Iraq between 2008 and 2010. U.S. and Iraqi officials agreed that too many of the reconstruction efforts already in place were ad hoc and did not provide enough of a critical mass of the necessary essentials. In response, USIP convened and facilitated working groups at the local, provincial, and federal levels to prioritize needs, develop strategic plans, and mobilize resources. The project did elevate the visibility of internally displaced person and refugee issues in Diyala. It did increase communication horizontally, within the province among the executive, legislative, civil society, and security forces and between U.S. and provincial Iraqi governments. It was less successful in improving communication vertically among the local, provincial, and federal Iraqi governments.

In the end, pilot projects and target communities were identified and comprehensive plans were drawn up, but resources to implement these plans were not secured. The push to obligate $200 million within the fiscal year overshadowed and overwhelmed the project, which fizzled to an inauspicious ending.

Chapter 3 presents the third case, a series of dialogue meetings between Kosovar Albanians and Serbs to promote constructive engagement and ultimately peace between the two communities in Kosovo. These meetings were held between 1998 and 2002 and involved a variety of officials, politicians, intellectuals, civil society leaders, and youth. One of the early meetings was held in Virginia and resulted in the Landsdowne Declaration, which was referred to in Kosovo for many years after the meeting. The discussion focused on the political process, on economic reconstruction, revitalization, and reform, and on strengthening civil society. The task was to project what kind of Kosovo the participants wanted to see in five years, to assess where Kosovo was at that time, and to define what needed to be done to get from the current situation to the desired future state. One in a series of follow-up meetings focused on the creation of an NGO, the Council of Professionals, which would institutionalize interethnic cooperation.

Subsequent meetings focused on training workshops, which led in turn to facilitated dialogues between Serbs and Albanian Kosovars on interethnic coexistence and coalition building. Among the outcomes was a series of documents that served as standards for cooperation, dialogue, good governance, and economic and social reform in Kosovo. The dialogues also made Kosovo a safer, more peaceful place and brightened its future prospects.

Chapter 4 presents two cases on religious dialogue, one between Israel and Palestine, the other in Colombia.

The Alexandria process consisted of sustained dialogue among Muslim, Christian, and Jewish leaders from Israel and the Palestinian territories beginning in 2002. It was launched in response to the second intifada in 2000, during which religious leaders concluded that a peaceful settlement of the Arab-Israeli conflict required active engagement of religious institutions and leadership. The Alexandria Declaration, which called for a religious peace, was approved by the two secular leaders at the time, President Yasser Arafat and Prime Minister Ariel Sharon. Overall, the Alexandria process had only limited impact on the larger conflict, but it did establish important interfaith relationships that have endured and provided the basis for interfaith intervention at critical moments. It also organized several important interfaith initiatives, particularly between Israeli Jews and Muslims. In addition, it led to the creation of a successor organization, the Council of Religious Institutions of the Holy Land, which brings together the three faith communities on a regular basis and helps organize joint interfaith action.

In Colombia, religious women from both Catholic and Protestant communities were brought together to engage in joint activities to promote peace. Beginning in 2006, USIP staff discovered that women involved in peace efforts through their religious communities were organizing exciting initiatives and were eager to engage more deeply in ecumenical work. Previously, most of the peacemaking by the two faith communities had been managed by men. Since 2008, the process has involved women. The dual goals of the initiative are to build ecumenical relationships to create a broader movement of faith-based peacebuilders and to affirm and strengthen the role of women in peacebuilding.

Chapter 5 focuses on efforts to promote peace in Colombia. Between 2008 and 2010, USIP helped organize a series of dialogue meetings, which were held in both the United States and Colombia. Participants included peace and human rights groups from Colombia, U.S. government officials, and American NGOs. These meetings created a space for civil society leaders to discuss, define, and articulate strategies for peace in Colombia; to build relationships and networks to put peace on the agenda of U.S. NGOs and American policymakers; and to ensure that U.S. policies better supported Colombian efforts to secure peace.

One goal of these meetings was to encourage the U.S. government to give higher priority to promoting peace in Colombia. Participants recognized, however, that designing policies to promote peace required clear direction from Colombian civil society organizations about what they wanted and how they wanted to get there. Not all the goals of the project were met. However, the dialogues did create and strengthen sustainable relationships, helped build capacity to contribute to peace, and provided a safe place where ideas could be floated, strategies discussed, consensus built, and initiatives vetted and launched. They also strengthened linkages, working relationships, and networks, and helped focus conversations within Colombian civil society on a national peace agenda.

Chapter 6 addresses the Niger Delta, a rich oil-producing region plagued by intense interethnic fighting and, more recently, attacks by armed militants against oil industry and government facilities. The area is also the site of two USIP-funded conflict management projects, dating from 1999 to 2007 and executed by Academic Associates PeaceWorks (AAPW). The first focused on a two-year facilitated dialogue among the three ethnic groups involved in long-term competition and conflict. The second brought together the various parties in twenty particularly conflict-prone local governments to work for nonviolent elections in 2007. Outbreaks of violence interrupted mediation, however, and the government's flawed peace efforts failed. The situation continued to change and required new creative solutions with each shift.

These meetings generated the creation of the Warri Peace Forum, named after the city where most of the violence occurred. Over time, Warri became a much more peaceful place. The process was not linear, but progress toward peaceful accommodation has been made.

Chapter 7 presents the final case study, Nepal, where a justice and security dialogue was initiated to bridge the gulf of mistrust between the civilian police and local communities. The long-term goal is to help Nepal enhance its public security and usher in a society that respects the rule of law. The processes include nurturing communication, cooperation, and recognition that justice and security are two sides of the same coin. Also involved in this program are the human rights community, the judiciary, other security and justice stakeholders, government at both local and nation levels, and the country's political parties. All these are engaged in finding joint solutions to shared problems.

Working with local facilitators, USIP helped provide the neutral third parties to enable these dialogues to progress toward mutual understanding and shared solutions. Local facilitators were able to gradually assume full control of the dialogue process, ensuring its local relevancy and self-sustainability. At the core of the program are facilitated meetings at which members of the Nepal police and civil society formulate, express, and discuss their concerns about the justice and security situation; develop ideas for tackling those challenges; and present those ideas to representatives of political parties and local government administration. The results of the local dialogue are then fed into the national policymaking process.

Conclusion

All the cases in this volume illustrate processes of facilitated dialogue. Several, including both Colombia cases, Israel-Palestine, and Nigeria, fit comfortably in the category of Track 2 diplomacy as well. Others—including those in Kosovo, Mahmoudiya (Iraq), Diyala (Iraq), and Nepal—are not conventional cases of Track 2 diplomacy, but they illustrate facilitated dialogue processes for resolving societal problems in conflict zones. Each of these included participation by officials as well as nonofficials, sometimes with a thin veneer of participating in a "personal capacity." USIP has found this Track 1.5 mix particularly fruitful in those situations that allow it to happen. These Track 1.5 efforts have tended to focus more explicitly on developing action plans for meeting interests that the participants come to recognize as common during the dialogue process. This interest-based approach may restore, build, or deepen personal relationships, but that is not necessarily their primary objective. In other cases—especially the instances of religious dialogue and the Niger Delta—personal transformation was a more explicit objective, quite apart from the creation of a common program of activity (though that often resulted as well).

This volume provides a collection of eight illuminating case studies in which USIP has used facilitated dialogue to promote peace. Lessons drawn from these cases have been instructive to USIP in its current and future peacebuilding activities. It is hoped that they will also be helpful to other individuals and organizations pursuing the same goals.

1

Iraq: Peace Initiative in the Triangle of Death

Rusty Barber

In June 2007, the head of USIP's office in Baghdad received a call from the USAID representative embedded with U.S. forces in Mahmoudiya, a rural district of 400,000 people in South Baghdad some twenty miles from the city center.[1] In the preceding months, U.S. and Iraqi forces had managed to drive back the various forces that had turned Mahmoudiya into a cauldron of violence so extreme it was commonly referred to as the Triangle of Death. Local tribal and government leaders had approached the 10th Mountain Division's combat team seeking support for an initiative that could seize the moment to turn a fragile security onto a path to sustainable peace. Could USIP help guide such an initiative?

This following chapter outlines the principal steps and approaches taken by USIP to assist the protagonists in Mahmoudiya organize and implement a peace initiative to end large-scale violence by bringing together key community leaders both inside Iraq and exiled in Jordan. Facilitated dialogue—face-to-face discussions enabled by third-party individuals—was the principal mediation tool, used in conjunction with training participants in conflict management skills. USIP's team consisted of its Baghdad field mission, led by deputy chief of party Zainab Shakr and author Rusty Barber, together with D.C.-based staffers Daniel Serwer, Julie Montgomery, and Jacki Wilson. Iraqi mediators Ali Neema and Dr. Saieb al-Gailani led a team of facilitators at the final conference, which established an accord among the region's tribes.

---

1. USIP has maintained a field office in Baghdad's Green Zone, staffed by Iraqis and Americans, since 2004. The author, Rusty Barber, served as chief of party from March 2007 to June 2008.

Background

Bounded on the east and west by the Tigris and Euphrates rivers, Mahmoudiya is a predominantly agricultural community, crisscrossed with farms and irrigation canals. It is also the road and rail gateway to Iraq's southern provinces: Shia pilgrims make their way on foot to the shrines in the holy city of Kerbala after passing through the region's namesake township of Mahmoudiya. Home to more than fifty Sunni, Shia, and mixed-sect clans, the Mahmoudiya region is dominated by tribes who have lived in relatively peaceful proximity to one another for hundreds of years. During his rule, Saddam Hussein planted munitions factories in the district and rewarded loyal army officers and Ba'ath cadres with land, creating a bulwark against a restive Shia population he feared might rise up in revolt, as it in fact did in 1991.

More recently, the region had descended into chaos following the U.S. invasion and the regime's collapse in the spring of 2003. A toxic mix of insurgents and terrorists had turned the district into a killing zone over which coalition forces had little effective control. Mahmoudiya became a haven for terrorists launching attacks in Baghdad; assassinations, beheadings, and sectarian warfare became the daily norm. The presence of armed bandits and IEDs (improvised explosive devices) rendered roads through the region impassible. Half of the district council members had been assassinated; local government had ceased to function; and traditional agriculture, markets, and transit systems had collapsed. In the fall of 2006, a massive car bomb detonated in Mahmoudiya's central market, killing fourteen people and reducing the market square to rubble. Once a bustling trading center for farm produce and equipment, Mahmoudiya township had become a ghost town. The district's population—Sunni areas in particular—suffered massive displacement, a large number of tribal chiefs fleeing to Jordan, Egypt, and Syria, from which locations some continued to provide support to insurgents. Resentment and deprivation expanded the rifts and fueled the violence.

The months leading up to the USAID officer's call had, however, seen improvement in the security situation. Several factors contributed to this change, most notably the tribal revolt against al-Qaeda. Hatched in Al Anbar province with U.S. sponsorship and franchised to other afflicted areas of Iraq, including Mahmoudiya, Sunni tribal militias were proving effective at routing their former allies. The U.S. military's shift in strategy to emphasize counterinsurgency tactics and the gradually improving capability of Iraqi forces also contributed to the change. By the summer of 2007, U.S., Iraqi, and tribal paramilitary forces—dubbed the Sons of Iraq—had succeeded in expelling al-Qaeda and were making progress subduing the militias. Local citizens confirmed that a measure of calm not seen in years had returned to the district. At the same time, they knew that the situation in Mahmoudiya—itself a reflection of the volatile political environment in Baghdad—remained highly combustible. Whatever window of opportunity for peace existed would be brief.

It was thus with a sense of both urgency and skepticism that the Institute's Iraq team considered the request for assistance. Several troubling questions presented themselves at the outset, not the least of which was whether the Iraqis would accept an American institute in the role of facilitator for a peace process in which the United States was itself a combatant.[2] Second, Mahmoudiya was home to a complex array of political, economic, and social problems, as well as a daunting number of tribal and civic stakeholders whose relationships with one another and with the Baghdad government were opaque to outsiders. Could USIP gain enough familiarity with these circumstances to play a competent convening role? Also unknown was how the Maliki government would react to such a sensitive enterprise on the capital's southern doorstep. The Shia leadership regarded the surrounding tribal areas with fear and hostility, particularly those populated by Sunnis, whom they considered sponsors of terrorism bent on returning the country to Ba'athist rule.[3] Without Baghdad's support—or at least its acquiescence—an already doubtful initiative would face an even tougher uphill climb. With these and other questions up in the air, the Iraq team decided to tentatively accept the request, taking cues from its Iraqi interlocutors to determine whether and how the Institute's resources might be put to use. One thing was certain: the Iraqis of Mahmoudiya would soon make it plain whether our presence was useful, harmful, or irrelevant.

A Conflict with Many Dimensions

The first challenge was to gain a grasp of the situation on the ground, no easy task in a place few outsiders, other than the military, had visited. The complexity was magnified by the number of tribes holding sway over various

---

2. Anti-American sentiment in Mahmoudiya was aggravated by a well-publicized case in March 2006 in which a fourteen-year-old girl was raped and, along with her parents, murdered. Four U.S. soldiers of the 101st Airborne Division were later convicted of the crime.

3. These fears were warranted; many officials were killed or wounded while attempting to venture out into Baghdad's rural districts. Others simply refused to go unless conveyed by military escort.

territories, their internal hierarchies, and their relationships with one another and with the central government.

A visit to the 10th Mountain Division's base on the outskirts of Mahmoudiya township afforded USIP its introduction to the district. A fifty-minute drive in a Humvee from downtown Baghdad provided a grim picture of decay wrought by decades of war, sanctions, and neglect. Makeshift shops with protruding rebar lined streets clogged with raw sewage and the debris of collapsed buildings. Shopkeepers and customers idly chatted in the rippling heat, drinking tea and largely ignoring our passage except to turn away from the dust the convoy kicked up. Tribal paramilitaries, their heads wrapped in *keffiyehs* against the sun and dust, manned occasional checkpoints, Kalashnikovs dangling at their sides. Forward Operating Base Mahmoudiya was a mini-fortress, its outer walls built of giant Hesco barriers filled with sand, its interior a labyrinth of sandbagged walkways between plywood structures. A trip to the latrine could result in one's becoming hopelessly lost.

Referring to a large area map that included detailed biographical data on the tribes and their leaders, Lieutenant Colonels John Laganelli and Joe Cantlin weighed in on the overall political and security situation in the district. They concurred that recent security gains presented an opportunity for peace if local leaders could organize themselves to take advantage of it. If USIP could assist, the officers intimated, the brigade would provide whatever logistical support it could.[4] Cantlin began by providing an introduction to Muayad Fadhil al-Shibly, the district's Shia mayor and principal advocate of a peace initiative. Short and round, with a voice that seldom rose above a high-pitched whisper, al-Shibly seemed an unlikely candidate for the role of peacemaker-in-chief. But his unimposing demeanor masked a canny political instinct coupled with a desperate desire to bring an end to the violence that had claimed so many lives and devastated the social fabric of his community. The survivor of several assassination attempts, al-Shibly was guarded twenty-four hours a day by U.S. and Iraqi forces. He confirmed that with the pressure off from terrorists and armed groups, an opportunity was at hand to gather the clan leaders together to try to reach consensus on how to bring stability to Mahmoudiya. The key, he whispered, was convincing Sunni sheikhs exiled in Jordan to participate.

---

4. Brigade commanders cited the hope that a successful peace process would reduce U.S. and Iraqi casualties as the rationale for allocating significant resources to support it. Privately, however, they also expressed the desire to leave Iraq on a positive note after a deployment that, by summer 2007, had claimed the lives of forty-three 10th Mountain soldiers.

These initial assessments were decidedly helpful in framing the basic situation in Mahmoudiya and the tensions that had led to it. For a more comprehensive picture, USIP enlisted the help of several of the Institute's Iraqi grantees in the South Baghdad region. These NGOs, which included a human rights organization, provided invaluable insight into Mahmoudiya's tribal dynamics, helping identify likely advocates and spoilers. Over the following weeks, the Iraq team made numerous trips to the district to gather views and information from local representatives and gauge their interest in a dialogue process. Without its own transport and protection during these encounters, USIP relied on the 10th Mountain for support—assistance the brigade gave unsparingly despite the added risk and strain on its resources.[5]

The picture that emerged was of a conflict with many fault lines: Shia versus Sunni, rural versus urban inhabitants, tribe versus tribe. Evidence of intergenerational conflict also surfaced as younger, more aggressive leaders sought to supplant the authority of their elders. Saddam's legacy of manipulation, however, seemed to be the underlying theme, Sunni clans having received the greater portion of government patronage over their Shia counterparts. In his quest to deter Iranian influence and gird himself against the Shia threat, Saddam had earmarked most of the plum government and military posts for Sunni tribes like the Janabi and the Jabouri. With his ouster, decades-old resentments erupted as privileged clans lost their sinecures and were driven off their lands. Bitter over their reduced lot, many struck back, sometimes joining cause with insurgents and al-Qaeda in hopes of muscling their way back into influence. Score-settling and revenge attacks fed a cycle of violence that showed little sign of abating. Weapons and money flowing in from foreign sponsors helped ensure that the machinery of violence was well lubricated. Frightened by the violence and attacks on infrastructure, central government ministries were reluctant to expend critical resources in the district, further aggravating tensions and adding to the daily misery of the population, which lacked sufficient water, power, and sanitation services. Other important aspects of the situation in Mahmoudiya were to emerge:

- The dominance of tribal culture in the region meant getting the clans to commit to a genuine dialogue process was a prerequisite to a durable peace. Tribal networks and traditional mechanisms for resolving conflict, however, had broken down.

---

5. A 10th Mountain escort during one of these trips sustained an IED attack. Miraculously, there were no casualties.

- By 2007, the ferocity of the violence had outstripped the population's capacity to absorb it. Desperate to find a path to peace so they could rebuild their devastated communities, citizens were ready to support their leaders in making hard compromises.
- Mahmoudiya's strategic location as a major transit point between Baghdad and southern Iraq, its mixed Shia-Sunni population, and its role as a terrorist breeding ground made it a good candidate for a peace initiative that could have broader impacts in the Baghdad governorate.
- Previous attempts to reconcile the clans in Mahmoudiya had quickly collapsed. It emerged that the exclusion of key Sunni chiefs, many of whom had fled to exile in Jordan, had compromised these efforts from the start.[6]

This last insight clarified al-Shibly's assertion about the importance of getting the sheikhs in Jordan onboard. The mayor proposed to lead a cross-sectarian delegation on a mission to Jordan to convince the exiled chiefs that a fleeting opportunity for peace—and thus an end to their exile—was at hand and to encourage their participation in a reconciliation process. He was under no illusions, however, and understood that these were just the first steps on a road that would take years to reach true peace and reconciliation. He was also aware that, successful or not, the initiative would have repercussions in Mahmoudiya. And though he was willing to put his life on the line to lead it, he acknowledged frankly that he had no idea how to organize it. Could he rely on USIP for help? The Iraq team, supported by USIP leadership, was ready to commit but remained bothered by the question of whether local stakeholders would accept American involvement in such a sensitive enterprise. "Look," a Mahmoudiya district councilman explained bluntly, "there isn't sufficient trust among the clan leaders to convene themselves and no one trusts the government to do it. You Americans have created a mess in Iraq, but in the current chaos you are the only force on the ground capable of providing security. The reality is, if you are not visibly involved none of the tribal leaders will trust the process enough to participate in it." Cantlin was more explicit: "I hate to get dramatic, but it's a life or death situation here—if this is successful, we'll never know how many lives were saved." Lingering doubts notwithstanding, the Institute would do what it could to support the mayor and his fledgling peace initiative.

---

6. The Amman sheikhs occasionally sent representatives to reconciliation meetings, but their participation was often disingenuous. As one U.S. commander wryly noted, "The sheikhs were sending one son to a reconciliation meeting and another son to an al-Qaeda meeting, just to cover their bases."

Together with tribal and civic leaders at an initial planning session in Mahmoudiya, the Iraq team sketched out a process that would commence with reaching out to the sheikhs in Jordan to encourage their interest in a peace initiative. If that interest proved forthcoming, and support from other key tribal leaders in Mahmoudiya followed, USIP could then lay the groundwork for an autumn conference bringing together the key sheikhs to agree on an action plan to restore stability to Mahmoudiya. Winning over the Jordan sheikhs was, however, only one of several hurdles that would have to be overcome. Everyone was assigned a role. Mayor al-Shibly and his colleagues would be responsible for establishing contact with the sheikhs in Jordan, getting the Baghdad provincial government onboard, and gathering the support of key figures within the district. USIP would engage the Maliki government, enlist support from the embassy and the international community, and serve as coordinator for the effort ahead. USIP would also design and staff the proposed conference. The 10th Mountain would provide security and transportation and assist with logistics for the conference.

Outreach to Exiled Tribal Leaders

In staging the outreach to tribal chiefs in Jordan, al-Shibly's first thought was to convene them as a group, with open discussion of the issues. Concerned that a big-tent format might quickly dissolve in acrimony, USIP suggested instead the delegation establish itself in a hotel and invite the exiled sheikhs to meet individually. This way, the leaders could take their measure of the initiative and air their personal views apart from their peers. The delegation could tailor its message to the individual concerns of the sheikhs while making the general argument that the tribes' welfare would be better served by participating in a legitimate peace process than by continuing to wage war from abroad. The sheikhs clearly had incentives to change course. Cut off from daily decision-making in Iraq, they were losing authority to younger, more bellicose leaders whose keenness for confrontation was only making things worse in the region.[7] Furthermore, with the Iraqi economy in shambles and their farms ceasing to produce income, the sheikhs were finding it increasingly hard to maintain themselves in pricey Amman.

Al-Shibly concurred with the individual format for the dialogues and set about assembling a delegation of tribal and civic representatives to credibly represent the key stakeholders and make an effective argument for peace.

---

7. Several tribal leaders expressed to the author their deep concern about these intergenerational conflicts and their tendency to exacerbate tensions in Mahmoudiya society.

His shrewd choices included four individuals who would form the brain trust for the initiative. District Council chairman Najm Dleemi, one of the few surviving council members, was a fair-minded politician with strong links to urban Shia. General Ali al-Mufraji, the Iraqi Army commander in Mahmoudiya, was a respected officer and vocal critic of sectarianism. Sheikh Fariq al-Ghereri was a local farmer and leader of a mixed Sunni-Shia clan, a position that allowed him access to both sides of the sectarian divide. The delegation was rounded out by Mohammed Lafta, a soft-spoken shopkeeper from Mahmoudiya township whose farm supply business had been destroyed by militants. His deep knowledge of the key tribal personalities in Mahmoudiya would prove invaluable to the process.

To ensure representation from the provincial government in Baghdad, al-Shibly and Sheikh al-Ghereri secured the support of the governor of Baghdad province, who prevailed on a senior provincial councilman to join the delegation. Getting the Maliki government onboard proved a much greater challenge, given its loathing for remnants of the former regime and their supporters. To complicate matters, two competing agencies claimed authority over national reconciliation and tribal affairs: the Ministry of Dialogue and Reconciliation (MODR), under Minister Akram al-Hakim and the inelegantly named but far more powerful Implementation and Follow-Up Committee for National Reconciliation (IFCNR), headed by Deputy National Security Adviser Safa Hussein. Ostensibly a high-level committee tasked with integrating the Sons of Iraq into the national security forces, IFCNR was regarded by many as a tool for Prime Minister Maliki to extend patronage to tribal factions in exchange for their political support.

Familiar with USIP and its work in Iraq, al-Hakim readily granted the Iraq team request for a meeting with the Mahmoudiya contingent.[8] He was skeptical of the chances of success but allowed that al-Shibly and his colleagues made a compelling argument for their cause. As long as the Jordan mission was kept discreet, he would back it, assigning a retired Sunni general to accompany the delegation as MODR's representative. IFCNR, by contrast, reacted frostily to any venture involving outreach to individuals it considered bent on overthrowing the government. A full-court press ensued over the summer to reassure wary committee members that the potential benefits to security outweighed the risks of appearing to compromise with insurgents. Al-Shibly and his Mahmoudiya cohort appeared repeatedly before the com-

---

8. Akram al-Hakim was among the senior Iraqi leaders consulted by the 2006 Iraq Study Group, a bipartisan commission organized by USIP at the request of Congress to review alternative strategies for concluding the war in Iraq.

mittee as USIP reached out to senior Iraqi officials to encourage broader government support.[9] U.S. military and embassy officials also leaned on their government contacts. The persistence paid off. Despite its misgivings, IFCNR acquiesced in allowing the project to proceed, with the caveat that the delegation make it clear to the Amman sheikhs that it did not speak directly for the Maliki government. The light was now green for the mission to Jordan to proceed. Meeting in late July, delegation members established three objectives:

- to acquaint the Sunni tribal leaders with recent positive developments in the overall security situation that had opened a window for dialogue among the clans;
- to hear directly their views and grievances, with a view to gauging their receptivity to a community-based peace initiative;
- to encourage the sheikhs' participation in a conference to restore trust among the senior tribal leaders and hammer out a plan to bring stability to the region.

To these, IFCNR insisted on adding a fourth:

- to win the sheikhs' support for a Mahmoudiya tribal council to resolve disputes, identify terrorists, and nominate recruits for the Iraqi police and army.

USIP offered to underwrite the cost of the trip and provide observers. A trip date of July 15 was canceled when Jordanian authorities refused to issue visas but the trip was allowed to proceed two weeks later after prodding from the U.S. embassy in Amman. Washington-based staffers Daniel Serwer and Julie Montgomery traveled to Amman ahead of the delegation to take a preliminary pulse of the exile community. Their initial soundings did not bode well. In a message to the rest of USIP's team, Serwer described encountering a wall of hostility from exiles furious over the American invasion, which had brought an inept and corrupt Shia government to power in their stead. Dialogue and reconciliation were very far from their minds, which appeared focused on resistance and revenge, an attitude that if maintained in one-on-one meetings might render our peace initiative dead on arrival.

---

9. This outreach included regular communication with IFCNR's deputy director, Bassima al-Sa'adi, a close Maliki adviser. Nicknamed the Dragon Lady by U.S. officials for her purportedly fierce sectarianism, the author credits her tacit support for the Iraqi government's restraint in allowing the Mahmoudiya initiative to go forward.

These concerns appeared justified when the delegation's invitations to talks initially met with silence. Two days passed before Turki al-Talal, the elderly and respected leader of the Gurtan tribe, finally broke the ice and agreed to a dialogue. Dressed in full tribal regalia, al-Talal arrived agitated and suspicious. He enumerated a number of grievances and repeated them over the following several days:

- The United States was responsible for a disastrous, top-down approach to democracy development that had given rise to identity-driven politics.
- The occupation had created a security vacuum that Iraq's neighbors were exploiting to advance their own agendas and sow discord among Iraqis.
- Coalition forces were unable or unwilling to stop attacks on Sunnis by Shia militias, and Iraqi security forces were conducting random, unlawful detentions. Fear for their personal safety kept the sheikhs from returning to Iraq.
- The Iraqi government's inattention to rural security and economic development had enabled terrorists and militias operating in those areas to proliferate.
- Iraqis displaced from their homes should be granted right of return, protection, and compensation.

Acknowledging that some tribal leaders from Mahmoudiya actively supported resistance groups, al-Talal strongly condemned al-Qaeda in Iraq (AQI) and voiced resentment at what he viewed as a tendency to uniformly brand Sunnis as supporters of terrorism. At the same time, he was clearly unaware of recent developments in Mahmoudiya, including the growing cooperation between the tribes and the security forces. The wisdom of bringing General Ali al-Mufraji along became evident as the commander detailed the progress of his forces in confronting AQI and the militias. He also described efforts to oversee the Iraqi police, whose ranks were infested with Shia militiamen. Most significant, al-Mufraji was able to provide information on the status of detainees held by coalition forces, a special concern for al-Talal and his fellow sheikhs. Since the beginning of the war, thousands of Iraqis suspected of insurgent or terrorist activity had been swept up by American and Iraqi forces and held indefinitely in camps scattered around Iraq. Many had been detained for years, often on vague charges with no indication of when their cases might be adjudicated. Scrolling through spreadsheets on his laptop, the general updated the Gurtan leader on the status of a number of his tribesmen in custody, including when court hearings were scheduled. Last, to deflect charges of sectarianism in Iraq's armed forces, he disclosed the breakdown of his officer corps, confirming a rough balance between Shia and Sunni officers. Other delegation members spoke in turn, each reacting to al-Talal's testimony and many sharing their own experiences of violence and loss. Sheikh al-Ghereri, speaking as a fellow tribal leader, movingly described the devastation to his farmlands wrought by war and economic collapse. General al-Mufraji concluded the meeting on a poignant note, reminding al-Talal that he was a Shia married to a Sunni with sons named Hussein and Omar, Shia and Sunni names, respectively. "Am I to make war on my own family?" he asked.

By the dialogue's end, the delegation had won over its first ally in the exile community in Jordan. Al-Talal pledged his support for the initiative and promised to press other sheikhs to meet with the delegation. Over the next several days, half a dozen tribal leaders presented themselves at the hotel, each more inclined at the outset to air grievances than to discuss ways to end the violence. Beyond serving as a third-party observer, USIP's role during these dialogues was to help nudge the parties over the bumps and conduct the debriefings after each encounter, during which USIP offered options for effective follow-up. In this, the Iraq team was greatly aided by the keen observations of the quiet shopkeeper, Mohammed Lafta, who seemed to know the backstory of each sheikh and tribe and provided valuable insights into their underlying interests and motivations. Occasionally, team members stepped in to cool things down when tempers flared. A particularly tense exchange between a Janabi sheikh and al-Mufraji threatened to get out of hand as the sheikh, his voice shaking with anger, accused the general and his troops of intentionally failing to protect his tribe from militia attacks. USIP staff intervened to recommend the rest of the delegation take a break to allow the two to continue privately. The harsh voices gradually subsided, and when the group reassembled, the sheikhs indicated they had come to an understanding, with General al-Mufraji promising to check on the status of a Janabi tribesman held by U.S. forces.

The delegation encountered its toughest and most articulate skeptic, however, with Ibrahim al-Shawi, leader of the Ubaid tribe. The author of several books published in Arabic and English and a PhD in industrial chemistry, al-Shawi was prominent in the Iraqi exile community, which made gaining his support a priority. He declined initially to meet the full delegation but agreed to a private discussion with al-Shibly at a nearby café. After an hour, the mayor arrived at the conference room, leading a still reluctant al-Shawi by the arm. Insisting we refer to him as doctor rather than by the tribal honorific of sheikh, al-Shawi was strident in his skepticism of self-proclaimed peace delegations—especially any that included Americans. He nevertheless accepted a seat and proceeded to excoriate the U.S. occupation that had saddled Iraq with a political system hardwired to promote sectarian conflict.[10] Pessimistic about the prospects for reconciliation in Iraq, he advised the group to start with a less intractable region than Mahmoudiya if it truly wanted to make progress toward peace. A plea to al-Shawi's sense of patriotism by the provincial councilman from Baghdad fell flat, provoking the doctor to retort that a government so riven with incompetence and corruption was in no position to appeal to his conscience.

The discussion had clearly hit a wall when General al-Mufraji strode in, having been roused from a nap by an urgent call from the author in the hope that his presence might turn things around.[11] Al-Shawi listened attentively to al-Mufraji's now-practiced presentation on operations against militants, the status of detainees, and officer corps composition. The general also provided details about the Iraqi government's plans to create three new army battalions made up of tribal recruits—a program valued by the sheikhs as much for the jobs it would create as for the enhanced security it would bring. Al-Mufraji reassured the doctor that these forces would be deployed in areas close to their tribal homelands where they could contribute to the security of their people. The change in al-Shawi's attitude wrought by the general's business-like demeanor and laptop of hard data was remarkable. In return for al-Mufraji's agreement to research the status of some three hundred Ubaid detainees, al-Shawi eased his opposition to the proposed peace conference and promised to facilitate communication with key Ubaidi contacts in Mahmoudiya.

With the promising outcome of the dialogue with al-Shawi, the delegation decided it had accomplished as much as it could have hoped for in Amman. A hardline element clearly remained embedded among the exiled sheikhs that could be expected to counter any bid for peace. Nevertheless, al-Shibly and his small delegation had succeeded in convincing a clutch of influential leaders that a broadly based peace initiative was afoot in Mahmoudiya that might be capable of bringing them in from the cold.

---

10. A reference to Iraq's current political spoils system by which government ministries and positions are divided up among the various ethnic and religious factions.

11. At thirty-five years old, al-Mufraji was one of the Iraqi Army's youngest and most promising generals.

Mahmoudiya: Cornerstone for Peace and National Accord

Anxious to capitalize on the momentum generated by the Jordan mission, the Mahmoudiya team pressed ahead with the effort to win the support of the remaining clan leaders. Of the hundreds of sheikhs in the district, thirty-four leaders whose presence at the conference would be essential to a successful outcome were identified. Engaging them face-to-face would take time, however, as many lived in areas still under threat. They would also need time to weigh the initiative's merits, factoring in the possibility that participating could land them on someone's hit list. To allow sufficient time to put the conference logistics in place and bring as many tribes onboard as possible, a conference date was set for mid-October, despite its proximity to the Muslim holy week of Eid al-Fitr. Senior Iraqi government officials would be invited to observe the proceedings in hopes that a positive outcome might motivate them to allocate more resources to the impoverished district.

As Mayor al-Shibly, Sheikh al-Ghereri, and others worked to enlist Mahmoudiya's clans, USIP staff in Baghdad and Washington shaped the agenda for a three-day conference. For help, the Iraq team turned to several of the Institute's more experienced Iraqi partners, individuals skilled in conflict management techniques and familiar with the unique characteristics of Iraqi tribal culture.[12] By virtue of their authority and experience, tribal leaders are natural negotiators and problem-solvers. The challenge was to create an environment that would enable them to exercise these abilities in overcoming the profound mistrust that had stymied their traditional mechanisms for resolving disputes. Rather than have the participants engage in a conventional format of speeches and declarations, the Mahmoudiya conference would combine training and facilitated dialogue to encourage the formation of specific community goals such as rehabilitating destroyed schools and hospitals, holding elections and getting the local economy back on its feet. Instruction in negotiation, mediation, and group problem-solving techniques would, USIP hoped, provide the sheikhs with a common vocabulary for overcoming differences that would carry over into the working groups. The working groups would tackle five issue areas: security, economy, governance, rule of law, and social well-being.[13] On day one of the event, each clan leader would be assigned to a working group charged with developing

12. In 2004, USIP established a program to teach conflict management techniques to Iraqi civilians. By 2009 the program had trained more than 100 individuals and established a network of Iraqi facilitators to undertake mediation initiatives in conflict areas around Iraq.

13. *Social well-being* refers to issues such as return of displaced people and refugees, education, health, pensions, and so on.

three goals to be achieved within three years. Day two would be devoted to developing and prioritizing courses of action the sheikhs would undertake to realize these goals. On day three, participants would reconvene in plenary to debate and ratify the results of their work and produce a comprehensive accord. This format incorporated three goals:

- to encourage the sheikhs to focus on solving current problems rather than on past grievances,
- to foster a collaborative environment in which they could begin to re-build trust, and
- to enable the sheikhs to take collective responsibility for stabilizing and rebuilding their communities.

The question of who sits next to whom in negotiations involving hostile parties is a sensitive matter requiring some forethought. To help navigate seating arrangements, USIP turned to the shopkeeper, Mohammed Lafta. Drawing on his extensive knowledge of the participants' biographies, Lafta worked closely with USIP staff to assemble the working groups to maxi-mize the potential for innovative and constructive thinking. The result was a delicate balance that emphasized geographic and sectarian diversity and minimized the risk of serious friction.

The conference's most distinguishing feature, however, was that it would be conducted entirely by trained Iraqi facilitators. Six men and one woman would guide the sheikhs in their deliberations, helping them shape their ideas and objectives, ready to step in should tensions get out of hand. They would be led by two unique individuals from opposite ends of Iraq's religious and social spectrum. Saieb al-Gailani was a prominent Sunni surgeon and former deputy health minister before being forced to resign after receiving death threats. His co-leader, Ali Neema, was a scrappy Shia peace activ-ist and district politician accustomed to moving around some of Baghdad's most dangerous neighborhoods. Together they would conduct the training portions of the event, oversee the plenary sessions, and support the work of the facilitators.

Meanwhile, the mayor and his team relayed the welcome news that all thirty-four of the senior tribal leaders had agreed to participate in the con-ference, including Abdel al-Qadr of the Humair, who would attend from Amman on behalf of the exile contingent. Al-Shibly credited the influence of the Jordan sheikhs in convincing the Sunnis to take the initiative seriously. As word spread about the impending tribal conference, so did tensions. Insurgents stepped up efforts to derail the process through intimidation. Two weeks before the conference date, USIP learned that two invited sheikhs from the western township of Yussifiya had been assassinated. The number of attendees would stand at thirty-two. The pressure was taking a toll on the Iraqi organizers, especially Mayor al-Shibly, who in spite of his central role was showing signs of having cold feet. Zainab Shakr spent many hours on the telephone lending a sympathetic ear and giving him encouragement.

In light of the escalating security threat, our plan to hold the event in Mahmoudiya had to be abandoned when no suitable site could be found in which to host and protect the participants. The Al-Rashid hotel, across from the Iraqi Parliament in Baghdad's Green Zone, was chosen instead. Once again, the 10th Mountain brigade stepped up to provide security and transportation, establishing a cordon around the hotel a week in advance with the assistance of Iraqi soldiers under General al-Mufraji. Bomb-sniffing dogs were deployed daily to sweep for explosives.[14] Most significantly, Cantlin and the brigade managed to secure funding for the event after convincing General David Petraeus of its importance.

On the first day of the conference, the tribal leaders arrived by U.S. military convoy, bleary-eyed from the dawn operation to collect and deliver them safely to the Al-Rashid. Al-Gailani opened the proceedings with an eloquent discourse on the challenge of overcoming differences, framing his remarks in the context of a shared Iraqi identity and reminding his listeners of the responsibility they bore as leaders to ease the suffering of their people. Like an Iraqi version of Phil Donahue, he roamed among the participants, microphone in hand, inviting them to introduce themselves and explain why they had come and what they hoped to achieve. This was nothing like the traditional *majlis*—tribal gathering—the sheikhs were accustomed to. As the session wore on, however, surprise and skepticism gave way to studied curiosity as al-Gailani instructed them on key principles of negotiation and group problem-solving.

Moving into their working groups with the facilitators, things were going smoothly as the sheikhs began work on identifying and prioritizing goals in their respective issue areas. Inevitably, the calm did not last. An altercation between two participants working on governance issues erupted into a full-fledged shouting match, one sheikh accusing the other of having mur-

14. These precautions were deemed necessary in light of the Al-Rashid's location beside an entry point through which large numbers of officials and their armed guards passed, often under lax security conditions. The bodyguard of a legislator is believed responsible for the April 12 suicide bombing of parliament.

dered members of his tribe. Al-Gailani and Ali Neema moved quickly to separate the two, taking each by the hand to cool off in the company of his acquaintances. Calm restored, the sheikhs resumed their deliberations.[15] By the conclusion of the first day, the working groups had succeeded in developing a solid set of fifteen goals, which were then negotiated and ratified by the sheikhs in plenary. Five of these were as follows:

- Establish conditions for free and transparent provincial and local elections based on an open list system.
- Restore the rule of law to Mahmoudiya through the creation of an independent judicial system.
- Provide for the return and protection of thousands of citizens displaced by the violence.
- Ensure that only an accountable security force, operating under government authority, maintained the right to bear arms.

Day two would be devoted to hammering out the specific actions the tribal leaders would undertake to realize their goals.

Arriving early the next morning, USIP was surprised to find the sheikhs gathered in a traditional tribal circle. A flare-up of violence in the district the night before had claimed yet more lives, and the tribal leaders were discussing how to deal with it. Also under discussion was the formation of a tribal council to follow up on conference outcomes and deal with the government's request for assistance in vetting recruits for the security forces. Some of the USIP staff and facilitators were concerned that time was being lost, but that missed the point: it had taken months to convene the leaders, and little more than a day of interaction for them to reestablish the capacity to work together. Their deliberations concluded, the sheikhs announced their decision to redistribute themselves among the working groups according to their geographic locations in the district. This rearrangement, which put them more directly into win-or-lose confrontations, lasted just twenty minutes before quarrels broke out, prompting them to request that they be returned to their original assignments.

The only serious disruption to the day's proceedings came from al-Mufraji—invited, accompanied by a U.S. military officer, to briefly observe from the sidelines—who had apparently grown frustrated at the pace of

---

15. Later in the day, with al-Gailani and several participants mediating, the two adversaries agreed to put aside their hostilities for the duration of the conference.

events. Commandeering a microphone, he threatened the stunned sheikhs with arrest if they failed to produce an accord that included a clear commitment to support the efforts of security forces in Mahmoudiya.[16] His outburst threatened to abruptly end the conference but for the quick intervention of the accompanying American officer who deftly escorted the Iraqi general from the room. After a period of panic among the participants, facilitators were able to reassert control of the agenda and work resumed without further incident.[17] By the end of the day, the tribal leaders had added to their list of goals for the stabilization of Mahmoudiya a corresponding list of action items. USIP staff worked overnight to produce a draft accord to be negotiated and, hopefully, signed by the sheikhs the following day in a public ceremony attended by senior government officials and the press.

The final day commenced with prayers led by a prominent local imam, who recited passages from the Koran emphasizing forgiveness and reconciliation. Negotiations over the final text were intense and sometimes contentious, but largely absent of rancor. USIP staff and facilitators shuttled among the various groups, helping hammer out an accord in time to meet the afternoon deadline. Press crews were already setting up their equipment to broadcast the signing ceremony when agreement was finally reached. The agreement—Mahmoudiya: Cornerstone for Peace and National Accord—was signed by all thirty-two senior tribal leaders before a large gallery of Iraqi and foreign press. General al-Mufraji, having overcome his agitation of the previous day, gave an interview to Iraqi television expressing confidence that the accord marked a major turning point in the struggle to bring stability to Baghdad province.

Elation over the success of the conference was tempered by disappointment that only a handful of invited parliamentarians and government officials turned up to witness the event. The tribal leaders craved official recognition for making what they regarded as a significant contribution to peace and security in one of the most violently intractable regions in the country. They also worried that if tangible results in the form of improved services to towns and villages did not flow quickly, public confidence would erode, threatening a return to mayhem. Efforts in the ensuing weeks to strengthen

---

16. Such support was to include identifying terrorists and weapons caches and providing local recruits for the army and police.

17. The author and Daniel Serwer met privately with the general to explain the process under way and why his interruption was counterproductive to an outcome likely to benefit his long-term security goals. Al-Mufraji cited the heavy casualties his brigade had suffered, some at the hands of attending sheikhs, for his outburst. He promised, however, to refrain from further interference.

linkages between local officials and the Baghdad central government to improve power and water supplies progressed at a maddeningly slow pace.

On the ground in Mahmoudiya, positive impacts of the accord were more visible. Thanks in large part to a public awareness campaign led by Mohammed Lafta with support from USIP and the embassy, word of the sheikhs' agreement spread quickly. Large billboards and posters erected throughout the district announced the accord and reprinted the sheikhs' commitments. USIP facilitators conducted a series of community forums to reach out to farmers, students, businesspeople, and women. Under the auspices of the new council, the tribes coordinated efforts to maintain security, resolve disputes, and gradually enable the return of displaced persons, including the sheikhs in Amman, most of whom returned to Mahmoudiya within months of the Al-Rashid conference. Mosques forced to close during the fighting were reopened, accompanied by worship services led jointly by Shia and Sunni imams. U.S. commanders and civic leaders reported a significant drop in casualties and attacks following the conference, and credited the tribal initiative with saving many lives. Perhaps most symbolically, Mahmoudiya's central market was reopened, an occasion marked by a procession of tribal leaders walking arm-in-arm through the town. For many, it was the first time they had been able to visit the town in three years.

Mahmoudiya, like much of Iraq, continues to experience incidents of violence and sectarian tension, a legacy of identity-driven politics that remains an unfortunate fixture in Iraqi affairs today. Large-scale, systemic violence, however, of the kind that engulfed the region from 2004 to 2007 has ended. Viewed in this context, USIP's four-month dialogue initiative was successful in helping the region's key leaders restore trust among themselves and assume collective responsibility for Mahmoudiya's security through a shared vision for its future. Prospects for a more durable peace in Mahmoudiya—and indeed throughout Iraq—now rest on whether local leaders and their counterparts in Baghdad can partner with one another to provide the nuts and bolts of effective governance: equitable distribution of essential services and economic development leading to job growth.

> We want to close this painful page of our memories, in which our children became accustomed to seeing daily scenes of killing and displacement . . . our houses and farmlands burned down . . . dead bodies floating on the surface of the canals.
>
> Now, as we are moving toward parliamentary elections, we are witnessing the Sunni voter choosing the Shia candidate . . . and this took place in my own tribe as well.

Finally, we seek to build a more humanitarian society in which the individual is secure within the family, the family is secure within the community, and the community is secure within the state.

— Sheikh Fariq al-Ghereri reporting on conditions in Mahmoudiya in March 2010

Lessons Learned

• *Let local facilitators take the lead whenever possible.*
The advantages of having indigenous facilitators take the lead in conducting dialogues among parties in conflict would seem obvious. First, they are culturally and linguistically better attuned than outsiders to the situation and therefore more apt to pick up on relevant nuances in speech and body language. Second, because they are local to the conflict they are in a better position to follow up with the parties involved. Last, harnessing the skills and experience of local facilitators builds the capacity of a population to solve its own problems in the future. However, whether due to a lack of experience or to insufficient perceived neutrality, otherwise competent local persons may be unable to play a third-party role, obliging outsiders to step in.

In the Mahmoudiya case, USIP facilitators were blessed to have both experienced and objective Iraqi facilitators available to lead the Al-Rashid conference. This was not fortuitous. In 2004, as Iraq's descent into widespread violence gained momentum, the Institute had trained a small cadre of Iraqis in the hope of creating the nucleus for an indigenous conflict resolution capacity. Thus, when the need arose for facilitators for the Mahmoudiya conference in fall 2007, it was to this seasoned group that USIP facilitators turned for assistance.[18] The Iraqi lead role not only helped inoculate the process against the shadow of occupation and anti-American sentiment, it also provided Iraqis with an inspiring example. After attending countless trainings and mediations led by foreigners, participants and observers said repeatedly how gratifying it was to watch Iraqis helping fellow Iraqis end violence through a structured process. Without the lead presence of the Iraqi facilitators during the Al-Rashid conference, it is doubtful the outcome would have been the success it is generally judged to be.

---

18. At the time of the Mahmoudiya conference, USIP's combined training and dialogue model as a tool for resolving conflict was new to Iraq. Also, it is important that none of the Iraqi facilitators involved were from the district.

The Al-Rashid experience convinced USIP that it had an obligation to go well beyond the handful of Iraqis it had trained in 2004. To that end, the Institute's training department, together with the field office, developed an Iraq-wide program to recruit, train and support a network of Iraqis capable of leading dialogue and mediation efforts at the local level. A similar program is under way in Afghanistan.

• *Focus on the future and use narratives of violence.*
For individuals and groups emerging from violent conflict, the tendency to focus more on the past than on solving current problems and looking to the future is understandable. It is especially common when wounds are fresh and victims have not had access to justice. Excessive focus on the past, however, can quickly deluge a dialogue process in acrimony and lead to collapse. As chapter 3 suggests, creating a structured opportunity for participants to share personal narratives can provide a constructive outlet for the anguish and anger they feel.

The Mahmoudiya conference, however, presented a dilemma. The extreme nature and stubborn persistence of the violence led the Iraq team to doubt its ability to manage discussion around it without risking a complete meltdown. At the same time, the facilitators recognized that jumping into an exercise to map out a future for Mahmoudiya with no acknowledgment of its recent trauma would be callous and, quite possibly, counterproductive. Sheikh al-Ghereri, a local organizer, was adamant that the agenda include an opportunity for tribal leaders to testify to the violence they had witnessed and, in many cases, engaged in. The compromise solution was to provide participants with an anonymous questionnaire asking them to describe their personal experiences and comment on the impact of the violence on themselves and their communities. The questionnaires were then copied and circulated among the entire group—an approach that seemed to work well. Anonymity allowed the sheikhs to be unusually candid and provoked considerable exchanges on the margins without the need for a full-blown discussion in the plenary.

• *Follow up and measure outcomes.*
The Mahmoudiya initiative that culminated in the Al-Rasheed conference can be characterized as a solid near-term success in that it enabled the tribes to reestablish communication with one another after a prolonged period of dysfunction. Progress toward peace in the long term, however, typically requires the facilitator to remain engaged, helping the parties to stay in contact

and encouraging follow-through on their commitments. Because of security and funding constraints, USIP was not able to remain as engaged with the sheikhs of Mahmoudiya as would have been desirable. However, through a public awareness campaign and facilitated dialogues targeting key elements of the population, the Institute was able to spread word of the accord and stimulate discussion on ways concerned citizens could hold the sheikhs accountable.

At the time of the Mahmoudiya initiative, USIP's means of assessing the impact on stability and security in the region were admittedly more qualitative than quantitative. A more systematic effort to collect data through local interviews, violence statistics, and incidences of tribal cooperation with security forces before and after the Al-Rashid conference would have been useful, albeit difficult to separate from trends already under way. Anecdotal evidence of the initiative's positive impacts on stability was nevertheless significant. U.S. commanders, for example, directly credited the Mahmoudiya initiative with a precipitous decline in troop casualties, and civic leaders documented a pronounced increase in intertribal cooperation to resolve pressing concerns such as the return of families displaced by the violence.

• *Document when possible.*
Iraqi facilitators, participants, and USIP staff involved in the Mahmoudiya process frequently lament the fact that no video documentation of the initiative—and particularly of the Al-Rashid conference—exists that could be incorporated into an educational video and disseminated both within and beyond Iraq. They argue that Iraqis would have benefited enormously from watching other Iraqis overcome differences, even amid appalling violence, to solve problems through structured dialogue. The presence of a camera during the more sensitive episodes—the meetings with exiled sheikhs in Amman, for example—would have been unthinkable. However, many of the tribal participants at the Al-Rashid event indicated that they would have welcomed discreet filming on the second or third day had it been sanctioned by all the participants.

2

Iraq: Facilitation in Diyala Province
Caelan McGee

The Diyala Local Solutions Project for Internally Displaced Persons (IDPs) was an attempt to coordinate the reconstruction efforts specifically for refugees that were under way in Diyala province from 2008 through 2010. Both U.S. and Iraqi officials identified that too many reconstruction efforts were ad hoc, providing one or two critical resources to a community but not enough of a critical mass of the essentials required for a community to settle or resettle.

In response, USIP convened and facilitated working groups at the local, provincial, and federal levels to prioritize needs, develop strategic plans, and mobilize resources. The project did enjoy some success in elevating the visibility of the IDP and refugee issues in Diyala. It also resulted in increased communication horizontally—that is, within the province among the executive, legislative, civil society, and security forces and between U.S. and Iraqi governments in the province. Success in improving communication vertically between the local, provincial, and federal Iraqi governments was less notable.

In the end, these working groups identified communities for pilot projects, developed comprehensive plans for the reconstruction of these communities, and yet were unable to secure the resources to implement. Some of the projects were eventually implemented by the U.S. military but lacked the partnership and contribution of provincial government to provide comprehensive solutions. The arrival of significant resources for IDPs in Diyala from the U.S. embassy and United Nations High Commissioner for Refugees (UNHCR) in 2009 became the most visible effort in the province, supplanting this resource-limited exercise in collaborative governance with a well-funded but unilateral housing construction effort.

The shortcomings of this project aside, a strong need for facilitated dialogue to support local and provincial governments in Iraq remains. Simple practices such as convening, agenda development, meeting facilitation, and note taking can increase the efficacy of nascent decentralized governments while serving the goals of transparency and accountability. In this way, simple facilitation of local government processes can contribute to stability and conflict prevention in a conflict environment.

Background

Diyala is sometimes described as a microcosm of all of Iraq. It is demographically diverse, with elements of virtually all ethnic and religious groups found elsewhere in Iraq. Its geographic location is literally at the crossroads of Kurdistan, Baghdad, and Iran, destabilizing forces from each spilling over into the province. The region has experienced protracted violence, strife, and displacement for approximately three decades beginning with the Iran-Iraq war. Extremist militias have migrated to this area as they have been pushed out of other regions in Iraq. The economy has suffered greatly from the destruction of infrastructure and the flight of professionals, and these effects have been exacerbated by a drought that has badly damaged the agricultural sector.

Like much of Iraq, among the greatest challenges facing Diyala is the severe lack of essential services provision. Many villages have been razed during conflict or in subsequent efforts to clear villages and palm groves of weapons caches and explosives intentionally left by militias to injure government and foreign forces. Water, sewer, and electricity infrastructure has been neglected or intentionally destroyed during warfare. The lack of suitable housing is consistently identified as a key challenge, with a need for more than 50,000 units throughout the province in 2008. Garbage piles up in the streets in all towns and cities and in some places open sewage runs through the streets and into the rivers. Health care is severely lacking. Many schools are damaged or lacking supplies and teachers, or both.

At least two major factors contribute to the continuing violence in the province: political wrangling, which plays on sectarian and ethnic differences to mobilize different militias, and the legacy of violence, which has resulted in deep interpersonal resentment and cycles of revenge. The two factors are often confounded with simple labels of sectarian conflict. It is true that many have taken up arms in the name of an ethnic or religious group (and then subsequently switched their allegiance, in some cases several times). These allegiances, however, have formed as regional and national players have sought to recruit and manipulate a base of power within Diyala.

Before 2003, sectarianism was present but was not a driver of violent conflict. Diyala's diverse populace lived intermixed and in relatively peaceful coexistence. On a day-to-day level, few people harbor deep resentment for another person or group because of theological, philosophical, or racial differences. Severe unemployment and a lack of essential services, however, tend to lead to desperation, which enables those seeking power to recruit and manipulate groups in the name of religious and ethnic differences. The same economic hardship makes it difficult to break these cycles of violence and revenge, because people have few opportunities for income other than those provided by militias and little else to do than focus on their loss and suffering.

One political factor that threatens the stability gains in the province is the latent conflict around the border and jurisdiction of the Kurdistan Regional Government (KRG), especially in Khanaquin. Already much of the north and northeast of Diyala is de facto KRG, and administration and service provision is from Sulaymaniyah and Kirkuk. In 2008, Iraqi Security Forces representing Prime Minister Maliki and the Iraqi central government and the Pesh Merga troops of the KRG had several standoffs. Unresolved border disputes remain. This tension adds to an already volatile environment and comes as the buffer of U.S. military forces is being withdrawn. Any number of sparks might ignite smoldering tensions between Baghdad and Erbil.

Refugees and Displaced Persons as a Threat

After Baghdad, Diyala has the greatest number of displaced people. Of the approximately 2.8 million in Iraq in 2008, 19 percent originated in Diyala. The displaced moved from Diyala to many other provinces, but 80 percent moved within the province. Of those who did leave, Shi'ites tended to move south to the provinces of Baghdad, Basra, and Wasit, and many Sunni left the country. Sunnis also came in large numbers to Diyala from the south and west, especially from Baghdad, but also from Kerbala, Anbar, Wasit, and other places. An estimated 25,000 Diyala families—150,000 individuals—remained displaced in 2010.

Displacement from and within the province has a long history. During the time of Saddam Hussein, thousands of families were displaced, especially Kurdish in the northern regions. Several hundred more families were displaced between 2003 and 2005 during U.S.-coalition anti-insurgency campaigns. The heaviest wave began shortly after the bombing of the Samarra Mosque in 2006. The most cited reasons for displacement were forced evacuation, threats of violence, and general fear of violence.

Some returns are occurring, especially as security situations improve. As of late 2009, approximately 8,800 families had returned to their homes. A significant wave of returns occurred in 2005, consisting largely of Kurdish families returning to the northern areas of the province, especially Khanaquin. Another significant wave, approximately 3,000 families, returned in 2008 after successful efforts by coalition, Iraqi, and Sons of Iraq forces to remove al-Qaeda in Iraq and other militia forces.

In polls conducted by the International Organization for Migration (IOM) and United Nations (UN), refugees were asked whether they wanted to return home, relocate somewhere else, or settle where they were. Approximately 80 percent of respondents in Diyala and Baghdad indicated that they wanted to return home. In the southern provinces, a greater percentage indicated a desire to resettle in place.

The greatest needs for those displaced include shelter, food, and health care. Approximately 20 percent live in temporary housing such as makeshift huts and tents, which is substantially higher than in most places in Iraq. About 50 percent live in rented housing, but many renters responded that the sustainability of their renting situation was uncertain. The remaining are living in public housing or with relatives, or are squatting on military bases.

Although generally food shortage is not a problem, the administration of ration cards is complicated and difficult, and the transit to and from marketplaces is especially difficult given unsafe or onerous checkpoints. As a result, a higher percentage of the displaced (approximately 27 percent) are suffering from an effective shortage of food compared with the rest of Iraq.

Assisting Nascent Provincial Government

Through 2009, the provincial government of Diyala had seen little success in preparing effective provincial budgets and work plans and in providing essential services. Despite special federal provisions that authorized a rollover of provincial funds for regions that experienced protracted violence and chaos, such as Diyala and Ninewah, and despite severe needs, the provincial government in Diyala consistently obligated only a small portion of its annual budget to service delivery and capital improvement, almost all expenditures instead going to salaries and operational costs.

As in many regions in Iraq, a structural and functional disconnect remains between the provincial government and the central ministries. Examples abound of capital investment projects—such as the construction of new schools, water treatment plants, and irrigation pumps—that sat unused due to lack of operation and management funds that come at the discretion of ministries. Many of these projects then are looted and resold or stripped for parts, or just sit idle and degrade over time.

Structural and functional disconnects between the provincial council and the local government—*qada* (district) and *nahiya* (town)—councils are also not uncommon. There is no formal mechanism by which lower-level executives or legislators can communicate or advance objectives to the provincial government. There appears to be a lack of understanding of the roles and responsibilities, both horizontally in terms of the difference between executive and legislative bodies, and vertically among the nahiya, qada, and provincial governments. In this absence of clarity and responsibility, it also appears that the executives, the governor, and *qam aqams* attempt to manage their jurisdictions unilaterally and with limited success.

Designing the Process

In November 2008, the staff of the USIP Baghdad office were approached by several who identified IDP return and reintegration as an issue of critical need in Diyala. Those who sought help included a local parliamentarian, the U.S. Provincial Reconstruction Team (PRT), and representatives of civil society organizations working in the province. Because one of the central challenges to return and reintegration is tolerance and coexistence, these actors requested USIP's assistance in conflict resolution.

A series of interviews and research were lined up to prepare a situation assessment, which included identifying key issues related to coordinating refugee return and reintegration. It also highlighted the need for conflict resolution for communities in the midst of a migration, and recognized USIP's limited ability to safely and meaningfully assist communities in the midst of active conflict. Instead, the assessment focused on suggestions for how to structure a dialogue within and among local, provincial, and federal governments—to include the U.S. government—to improve the provision of essential services and reconstruction projects.

The assessment was reviewed by an assembly of Iraqi federal government officials, including ministers of relevant ministries and members of parliament. With some changes to the initial design, the group endorsed the assessment, agreed on the principles of the project, and committed to participate in a three-tier process to coordinate IDP return projects. This three-tier approach included convening three working groups or committees, each of which represented one tier.

The executive committee included federal officials such as the minister of displacement and migration, a parliamentarian from Kirkuk, and the director of the Implementation and Follow-Up Committee for National Reconciliation (IFCNR). The goal was to provide authority, oversight, and guidance, and help expand the pool of resources available for IDP return projects in Diyala.

The steering committee consisted of provincial officials—members of the provincial council and the executive administration, directors general of relevant ministries, commanders from security forces, representatives of civil society, as well as representatives from the U.S. PRT and the U.S. Army Civil Affairs and Psychological Operations Command unit of the battalion assigned to Diyala. The purpose of this committee was to decide which communities would host pilot projects for comprehensive redevelopment, and to coordinate among the actors, particularly to share the burden of funding.

The working groups were composed of local actors, including the *qam aqam* (mayor), members of the local council, local ministry employees, and local security commanders. These groups were convened in the communities selected by the steering committee and were tasked with developing detailed reports on migration trends and a prioritization of critical needs for services that would support return and reintegration. The group that originally reviewed and ratified the structure suggested in the assessment became the executive committee.

Setting the Stage: Building Cooperation

USIP first tried to convene the provincial steering committee. This process was delayed significantly by the 2009 provincial elections and the almost complete turnover in provincial government. In the interim, USIP was invited by provincial government and the PRT to convene the Diyala Dialogue, a visioning and strategic planning process for the newly elected government.

In a two-day workshop, designed by USIP and the PRT and delivered by USIP-trained Iraqi facilitators, the officials ranked the challenges to the stability of the province, set targets for improvement within the current term of office, and drafted this vision into the Diyala Declaration, which was ratified by consensus. This agreement highlighted IDPs as among the critical challenges of the province, and helped USIP gain the trust of provincial officials as an organization that could provide independent facilitation on provincial issues.

Convening and Strategic Planning

Once the provincial government was established and USIP and its partners had gained credibility, a group was convened that would become the steering committee for the IDP Local Solutions Project. The group numbered almost twenty and included broad representation from the provincial council, governor's office, several directors general, and the provincial director of the police. Representatives of the PRT and the U.S. military civil affairs unit were ex officio members of the group.

Meetings were initially frustrating for both USIP facilitators and participants. Many local officials arrived with expectations of big development resources to be spent at the discretion of USIP—the legacy of extensive but sadly ineffective spending by U.S. military and civilian programs. Only after several discussions did participants gain confidence that there were adequate sources of funding in the province, from both the government of Iraq and the U.S. government, and that with coordinated leadership, all of these sources could be tapped to provide comprehensive reconstruction for refugees in selected pilot communities.

Committee members were also somewhat impatient with procedural tasks the facilitators had introduced. For example, the steering committee was to define criteria for identifying and selecting communities that would benefit from pilot projects. Defining criteria collaboratively, and doing so before selecting communities, was a tool not only for fairness, transparency, and accountability, but also to avoid jealousy and potential conflict in recipient communities. Some committee members understood the importance of procedural rigor, others resented the time and energy these efforts required.

Moving from Planning to Implementation

Once operating protocols that defined the steering committee mission, structure, and decision-making mechanisms were in place and communities were identified for pilot projects, committee members were energized to develop concrete plans for action and pursue contracts for provision of essential service. Participants spoke with excitement about the process as a new model for intragovernmental cooperation and planning. Unfortunately, the project would soon face trouble activating the local and federal actors and maintaining momentum at the provincial level, and would eventually be overwhelmed by a well-funded effort of the U.S. embassy and the UN.

Initially, local facilitators faced resistance. Local officials wanted to steer development projects to different neighborhoods than those the steering committee selected. Some evidence indicates that local officials' motivation included personal gain or nepotism in their attempts to redirect projects to different communities. The tiered structure of the committees served its purpose, as the authority of the steering committee served as a backstop to keep the project on course and focused on the selected communities. When local officials threatened to block progress, the steering committee indicated that it would simply move on to select another community in another district, after which local officials capitulated and even cooperated. Later, when the local working groups came back with lengthy wish lists, many of which would not serve refugee populations specifically, the steering committee returned the lists and insisted on more focused and appropriate lists of needs and desired assistance.

Although the steering committee was successful in monitoring and guiding the local working groups to develop plans for reconstruction, it was much less successful in budgeting, securing, and allocating resources to reconstruction projects. Ministry funds were difficult to access, both because ministry spending priorities and discretion were still very much centralized in Baghdad and because local officials were neither suitably experienced nor eager to lobby for additional funds from their superiors. In addition, although the steering committee reached consensus about priority projects, no mechanism existed to reconcile this with the severely dysfunctional provincial budgeting and planning processes that identified different priorities.

Competing Efforts

The goal was for the executive committee to provide direction and authority under just such circumstances. However, the USIP-convened executive committee was supplanted by the High Committee on Diyala, created by the prime minister's office and ministerial Cabinet Order 54. This committee, chaired by the director of IFCNR, was to be part of a three-tiered process with federal, provincial, and local committees to streamline reconstruction efforts in Diyala and focus on refugee return and reintegration. The IDP Local Solutions Project was identified by the chair as the inspiration and model for the High Committee.

It was initially hoped that the establishment of the High Committee would provide the necessary authority, resources, and political coverage for the pilot projects, especially given that the prime minister's office allocated a significant fund of resources for compensation for the displaced. Unfortunately, the High Committee did not embrace the recommendations of the steering committee and the local working groups, nor did it develop specific plans of its own for comprehensive reconstruction processes.

Also, the oft-cited pool of funds under the discretion of the High Committee never materialized. Conventional wisdom at the time was that the treasury was blocking the release of these funds, because IFCNR was seen as a privately established, unofficial committee of the prime minister whose purpose was gaining political influence, especially in rural, tribal communities. Indeed, the High Commission did become the running platform for its chair, the director of IFCNR, who would go on a year later to be elected to parliament from Diyala in the 2010 national elections.

In mid-2009, subsequent to Order 54 and the establishment of the High Committee on Diyala, the U.S. embassy and UNHCR announced a $200 million effort for housing reconstruction for refugees in Diyala. This and the IDP Local Solutions Project initially seemed like complementary efforts, where embassy and UNHCR resources could be married with the community-based, provincially ratified plans.

The members of the provincial steering committee of the IDP Local Solutions Project offered themselves and their work as a functioning framework with which to partner for such tasks as selecting communities for housing projects. Participants warned both the High Committee and UNHCR representatives that there was a risk of jealousy among the communities selected for housing projects. Worse, without local knowledge, provincial officials warned that if initial places for housing projects were not selected carefully, housing construction could be stopped by violence in unstable and not-yet-ready communities. As an alternative, the steering committee offered the two communities they identified as pilot project communities as ideal candidates for housing construction, which would also contribute to the Local Solutions Project's goals of shared, comprehensive reconstruction.

Instead, the U.S. embassy–UNHCR housing effort relied almost exclusively on the recommendations of IFCNR under the auspices of the High Committee on Diyala to select communities for housing projects. This resulted in three unintended consequences.

One, the first communities selected for projects by UNHCR proved to be volatile and unstable, with jealousy over the siting of housing projects leading to threats of violence. The first construction projects were shut down midstream.

Two, the provincial government was left out of all planning efforts. This resulted in embarrassing oversights, such as the construction of new houses for which there was no electricity supply or water-sewer connections, partly because the directors general and relevant ministries were not included in the project planning. This was also a missed opportunity to build the capacity of local government. Rather than funneling development resources through the provincial government, the reconstruction projects were implemented by internationals, and thus bypassed the opportunity for decentralized governments to develop experience, credibility, and "muscle memory" for effective governance.

Three, in the push to obligate $200 million within a fiscal year, the IDP Local Solutions Project was overshadowed and overwhelmed. UNHCR and U.S. embassy officials in charge of the Diyala efforts expressed legitimate and likely accurate concerns that working with a collaborative process such as the Local Solutions Project would slow the initiation of housing construction. In this author's opinion, efforts to marry collaborative decision-making, improve governance, and the speedy construction of housing were not mutually exclusive. Indeed, the U.S. embassy, UNHCR, and High Committee did learn some of these lessons after the first unsuccessful projects and engaged in some nominal consultation with local government as housing construction continued.

Unfortunately, the housing reconstruction reflected more the model of giving a fish rather than teaching to fish. Houses were constructed, and despite some design flaws (for example, one- and two-room houses too small for families, lack of connections to service) served an important need in the province. Unfortunately, it was yet another example of internationals doing the work rather than supporting local government in service provision. Indeed, the U.S.-UNHCR project has concluded and left the province, and Diyala provincial government still has little experience in implementing major reconstruction projects for the citizenry.

Also, the rapid allocation and expenditure of so many resources to housing construction became a high-profile project that overshadowed other efforts. Participants in the Local Solutions Project, especially the steering committee, viewed the resources available to them through the provincial council and ministries as a pittance and difficult to obligate, were also unable to tap into the U.S., UNHCR, or High Committee funds, and eventually expressed frustration and fatigue, and the IDP Local Solutions Project fizzled out inauspiciously.

Outcomes

Although the IDP Local Solutions Project did not achieve its substantive goals, it did achieve several procedural ones.

Throughout the Diyala provincial government at the time, severe dysfunction and lack of communication among the branches of government were standard. The flurry of activity and initiatives of provincial councilors and the governor and security commanders was consistent, but the majority of these efforts were both personality-driven and solitary. Too frequently, provincial councilors would not be aware of parallel and similar initiatives. The Local Solutions Project expanded and improved communication horizontally, across branches of the provincial government, and with U.S. government counterparts in the province, the Provincial Reconstruction Team, and the battalion.

The project also offered a model for strategic planning that included basic but often missing tools for decision-making, such as inclusive convening, agenda planning, meeting facilitation, note taking, and written records of deliberations and agreements. Appreciation for these innovations could be seen in the consistent attendance by participants in the facilitated sessions, many of which lasted more than one day, a feat often difficult to achieve in Iraq. The participants expressed gratitude and continued to request USIP's assistance even though USIP had little to offer except the ability to convene and facilitate sessions, as well as some access to international funders.

Efforts to improve vertical communication and working relationships within provincial government saw some, albeit limited, success. Several participants indicated that it was through this process that they first worked in tandem with their district and town counterparts.

The project elevated the profile of IDP issues in Diyala. However ineffective the project may have been with respect to its initial goals of streamlining and expediting comprehensive reconstruction projects, the chair of the High Commission on Diyala attributed the motivation and structure for the High Committee and Order 54 to USIP and the project.

The local facilitators became some of the most experienced and skilled in the USIP-trained Iraqi network. Early in the process, mistakes were typical of the inexperienced. For example, rather than moderating discussion among stakeholders, facilitators tried to answer questions directly and to engage with participants during meetings. By the end of the process, the same facilitators spent more energy on meeting design, preparing participants before meetings, and used a lighter touch during meetings and more strategic interventions when facilitating meetings. This capacity for keeping discussions on track and decisions on record continues to offer some incremental value added to provincial governance.

Lessons Learned

The IDP Local Solutions Project can boast several procedural gains, though few substantive ones. Some of the lack of success can be attributed to the myriad difficulties of working in a conflict zone. The short tenures and high turnover of expatriates involved in reconstruction, the lack of communication and collaboration among international NGOs, and the difficulty of operating in dangerous environments all make any governance and reconstruction projects difficult. Additionally, in retrospect, some things if done differently might have enhanced the success and impact of the project.

USIP and the facilitation team were unable to regularly and frequently convene meetings at all three tiers: local, provincial, and federal. Each meeting required considerable logistic and security planning and often was subject to the busy and changing schedules of the participants. USIP also worked with a small team of only one expatriate and three local facilitators that was, because of its size, unable to manage tasks at multiple tiers simultaneously. The work of one tier (such as the provincial steering committee) would thus be held up until a task by another tier (such as the local working groups) was completed. This lack of momentum sapped participant resolve and commitment. Given the circumstances and the resources available, speeding up the process by holding frequent (such as weekly) meetings, and thus building and maintaining momentum, were not realistic. A relatively complicated facilitated dialogue process such as this should either be resourced appropriately or scaled back.

• *Facilitating across languages and cultures*
Experience indicates that in Iraq, small group work is often more effective than plenary discussion, especially early in a workshop. Participants often used early plenary sessions to grandstand or had difficulty staying focused on the tasks at hand. During such speeches, almost invariably at least one participant offered strong words, which were taken by another as outrageous

and/or offensive. In response, the offended participants responded with audible harrumphs, left the room in outrage, or talked all at once.

By contrast, small groups of three to eight people, with clear instructions, were often able to stay on task and report with constructive ideas and suggestions. The need for clear and detailed instructions and specific examples cannot be overstated. Most effective were worksheets and templates that participants were tasked with completing, or other hands-on exercises in which participants were expected to develop a specific product. These exercises can be very simple, consisting of just a few questions and guidance statements. Concerns that such exercises, especially the use of worksheets and sticky notes, would be received as patronizing or gimmicky by high-ranking elected officials were unfounded. In contrast, participants expressed appreciation for "well-structured exercises."

This is not to suggest that plenary sessions should be avoided. Indeed some plenary work is needed to initiate and set the tone for a conference. Also, in Iraq the expectation is that higher-ranking officials will offer opening remarks, often with at least one opportunity for a leader from each religious sect or ethnic group to speak. These statements can take time, often more than an hour, and frequently consume the entire first morning of a meeting. Attempts to abbreviate these sessions met with mixed success, and seemed to depend on the degree of trust and positive working relationships among the participants. The more tension in a group, the more difficult it was to avoid long speeches, even though they were likely to inflame and agitate.

Once participant tempers flared, a facilitator could do little to regain control. In fact, appeals for the group to regain composure often meant only that yet another person was speaking with a raised voice and adding to the energy of discord. Once past the tipping point, the most effective strategy was for the facilitators to begin packing up and leaving. Participants—in certain cases—would then focus on the facilitators rather than each other, appeal that the facilitators stay, return to the discussion, and sometimes apologize to each other.

One strategic decision faced several times during workshops was whether a local-national or expatriate facilitator should moderate discussion, and if so, when. Local facilitators can speak the native language, which is not only more engaging for participants but can also reduce the time consumed by half or more, especially when consecutive translation is used. Local facilitators are also able to pick up on small cues and nuances of behavior and word choice that foreigners often miss.

In several cases, however, local facilitators asked foreigners on the facilitation team to take over, especially when participants were resisting the design of agendas, exercises, and discussions. Whether out of politeness, respect, or other reasons, contentious participants often were more willing to engage in structured exercises when a foreigner delivered instructions and moderated discussion. This raises interesting and difficult questions about the ethics and implications of foreigners placing themselves in charge of conversations. For international interveners and development professionals, it also highlights trade-offs between achieving near-term results and building longer-term capacity among local nationals.

• *Facilitation as conflict prevention*
The limited success of the IDP Local Solutions Project does not negate how critical facilitated dialogue is to Iraq's emerging decentralized democracy. Many provincial and local governments are peopled with well-intentioned but inexperienced leaders. A democratic, decentralized system of decision-making and governance is new, foreign, frustrating, and slow. The inherent inefficiencies of a democratic system are exacerbated when inexperienced officials have difficulty staying on track in a meeting, not to mention in building on past discussions for which there is no record.

Building capacity for facilitated dialogue is a relatively simple and inexpensive way to improve the efficiency of provincial and local governments. Facilitation in the form of inclusive convening, agenda development, meeting management, and note taking can help these governments make better-informed, more collaborative decisions, and do so more quickly. Although no panacea, facilitation can incrementally help government be more effective in engaging constituents, delivering services, and improving the quality of life in Iraq's war-torn communities. Given the low level at which these governments function, this incremental value can be substantial.

3

Kosovo: Promoting Ethnic Coexistence
Daniel Serwer and George Ward

This chapter describes an effort that took place between governments and civil society. The training sessions and facilitated dialogues were part of a wider USIP effort to apply knowledge to conflict situations, demonstrating utility as well as intellectual capability. In general, the goal was to discover and exploit nonviolent options for conflict resolution. No single theory lay behind the effort, however. Those involved were practitioners of interest-based negotiation.

Background

The Serbian-Albanian conflict in Kosovo is a long-standing one but boiled into war only late in the 1990s, the last in a series of four conflicts (Slovenia, Croatia, and Bosnia came earlier) associated with the breakup of former Yugoslavia under the autocratic rule of Slobodan Milosevic. Contrary to widespread belief in the region, the conflict is not properly traced to the Battle of Kosovo Polje in 1389, in which Serbs and Albanians fought together against the advance of the Ottomans, who also had Albanian and Serb troops on their side. The contemporary conflict is more properly traced to the late nineteenth-century rise of Serbian and Albanian nationalism, which re-emerged several times over the twentieth century and in particular after the death of Tito. The importance of the Battle of Kosovo Polje to the Serbs—much ballyhooed in recent times—in fact dates from the nineteenth century, when the poet Vuk Karadzic made it a glorious defining moment for Serb national identity. In 1878, the formation of the Prizren League became a defining moment for Albanian national identity and the effort to unify Albanian populations in Albania, Kosovo, Serbia, Macedonia, and Greece.

These two national (the term used in the Balkans for ethnic) identities are incommensurable, at least in Kosovo today. Serbian national identity is closely associated with the Serbian Orthodox Church; language is not the defining characteristic. Albanian national identity, however, is closely associated with the Albanian language; Albanians pride themselves on being of many religions. One cannot, nevertheless, be both Orthodox and Albanian in Kosovo, although it is possible to be Orthodox and Albanian in Albania or Catholic and Albanian in Kosovo. The Serbian and Albanian languages have different origins (Slavic and Indo-European, respectively) and are mutually incomprehensible, though not devoid of mutual influence. Mixed marriages are few and far between, and the offspring would have to choose between the two identities, even if they spoke both languages.

Coexistence fraught with constant frictions dominated Albanian-Serb relations from the late nineteenth century until the 1970s, when Kosovo gained from Tito the status of an autonomous province within Serbia and its own representative on the collective presidency of then socialist Yugo-slavia. The frictions grew thereafter. The Serbs say that they were harassed and chased out by the Albanians, who claim that the Serbs left for economic reasons. The percentage of Albanian speakers has in fact been increasing in Kosovo for centuries as Albanian-speakers moved north. Whatever the reasons, the Kosovo population changed from 67 percent Albanian in 1961 to somewhere between 80 and 90 percent Albanian in the late 1990s, (this uncertainty due to Albanians' not participating in the census of 1991).

Both Albanians and Serbs in Kosovo consider themselves victims of the other group. Milosevic rose to power in Serbia in 1987–88 promising to protect the Serbs of Kosovo from Albanian violence. He took away Kosovo's autonomy in 1989, leading to street demonstrations and violence as well as the organization of an unofficial Albanian parliament that declared the province's independence in July 1990, a decision confirmed by an unoffi-cial referendum organized by the Albanians. Ibrahim Rugova, leader of the Democratic League of Kosovo (LDK), was elected president of the self-declared Republic of Kosova in 1992. Milosevic expelled Albanians from government jobs, leading the Albanians to organize their own university, school system, health system, and other institutions parallel to the existing but largely Serbian official structure.

The United States intervened diplomatically for the first time in late De-cember 1991, when President Bush warned Milosevic that the United States would respond to any military moves the Serbs made against the Albanians in Kosovo. This so-called "Christmas warning" is generally credited with getting Milosevic to desist from military action against the Albanians, but he nonetheless used his police and Serbianized administration to repress Albanian political expression throughout the 1990s. The system is often said to have resembled apartheid, in that the Albanians and Serbs lived separate lives and a relatively small number of Serbs oppressed a relatively large number of Albanians, though the level of exploitation and violence was not comparable to South Africa's version.

Rugova stuck to a policy of nonviolent protest against the oppression of the Serbian administration as the Yugoslav Army attacked first Slovenia, then Croatia, and finally Bosnia. Milosevic's purpose in Croatia and Bosnia was to carve out definable Serb areas that could become part of Greater Serbia. But he was determined to hold on to all of Kosovo. Frustrated by the West's failure to deal with the Kosovo issue at the Dayton peace talks in 1995, impatient with Rugova's passivity, provoked by Serb abuses, and financed by Albanian expatriates, the Kosovo Liberation Army (KLA) emerged in 1996 with attacks on Serbian police and other officials. Thus the fundamental divide in Kosovo Albanian politics appeared between those who took up violent struggle and those who remained committed to nonviolence, a divide that corresponds in part to the split between the rural-based KLA and the urban movement centered on Rugova.

At about the same time, the late 1990s, a divide also emerged on the Serbian side. The Serbian Orthodox Church had supported Milosevic in his rise to power and hoped to obtain from him the return of extensive church lands in Kosovo (*metohija*) that had been expropriated by Tito's Communist regime. Kosovo is indispensable to the Orthodox Church because of its roots there in the twelfth century and the presence of hundreds of religious sites and monasteries dotted throughout what the Serbs refer to as Kosovo and Metohija. By the late 1990s, the church was realizing that Milosevic had no intention of returning its land and that his continuing repression of the Albanians and their now violent response was leading in a direction that would endanger the shrinking Serb population. Thus the church and its Kosovo Serb supporters (as opposed to Serbs in Serbia) became increasingly anti-Milosevic and interested in developing a modus vivendi that would enable Serbs and Albanians to coexist in a Kosovo under Serbian sovereignty.

The conflict between the Serbian authorities and the KLA escalated rapidly in 1998. In April 1998, 95 percent of Serbia supported Milosevic in a referendum against foreign mediation to solve the Kosovo crisis. KLA successes during the spring led to a Yugoslav Army offensive in the summer and the displacement of hundreds of thousands of Albanian civilians.

International civilian observers deployed in the fall encouraged many to return home, but the killing of forty-five Kosovo Albanians at Racak in January 1999 precipitated a U.S.-European effort at Rambouillet, France, to force the Serbs and Albanians into a peace agreement. The failure of this effort and Milosevic's refusal of a NATO ultimatum led to the beginning of the NATO-Yugoslavia war in March 1999 and the flight of thousands of Albanians from their homes into Macedonia and Albania. The war ended in June with withdrawal of the Yugoslav Army from Kosovo, deployment of a NATO force under a UN Security Council mandate, return of the Albanians, and displacement of 200,000 Serbs, Roma, and other minorities from Kosovo.

Phases of Facilitation

USIP engagement with Kosovo began in the spring of 1998, after Milo-sevic's military action against the Albanians in Kosovo had begun but before the NATO-Yugoslavia war. It is best described as Track 1.5 diplomacy—between government and civil society.

Single-Ethnic Programs

Veton Surroi, a leading Kosovo Albanian publisher, had invited USIP to conduct a training workshop in conflict management in Pristina for a distinguished group of Albanian leaders. Surroi knew of USIP from participating in an annual workshop for Balkan leaders USIP organized with ELIAMEP, the Greek foreign affairs institute. USIP staff members were unable, however, to obtain from the Milosevic regime visas to enter Yugoslavia. Rather than cancel the event, Surroi volunteered to send a group to Sofia for the workshop.

The group of twenty that arrived in Sofia did not include the relatively high-ranking political leaders that USIP had expected but rather was composed mostly of younger NGO staff, academics, and media representatives, as well as two interpreters. They ranged widely in their attitudes toward the growing violent rebellion in Kosovo. Most were frightened by it, not least because its success would mean that the guns of the KLA, not intellect, had triumphed. These mostly Pristina-based and university-educated Albanians did not look forward to a Kosovo dominated by a mainly rural movement. For the most part, they had envisaged an eventual triumph of Rugova's non-violent effort, a triumph that would empower NGOs, academics, and journalists more than a violent revolution.

Greeting the group as they got off the bus in front of the Intercontinental Hotel in Sofia was a simple gesture of hospitality and a good idea: it was taken—as intended—as a sign of respect. The group was not in the best of moods, having traveled through southern Serbia and crossed the border under the close eye of the Serbian police. They were delighted to discover that Sofia was an attractive city (relative to Pristina) and that they were staying in a more than decent hotel.

By the end of the first day, however, problems had surfaced. After eight hours of lectures, the group was anxious and edgy. The thinking had been that participants needed these lectures as a base before engaging in more participatory activities: simulations and discussions of their own situation. As interesting as some of the presentations were—the group was particularly impressed with Dr. Hal Saunders's presentation on peace processes—the day involved too much sitting and too little relevance to Kosovo. The entire next day was therefore spent in simulation exercises. The third day included an additional lecture by Dr. Saunders, but simulations continued.

These focused mainly on win-win situations, where gains for one side do not necessarily entail losses for the other. Balkan societies tend to assume zero-sum outcomes. A favorite regional joke—told by all the ethnic groups about the others—involves a farmer offered three wishes by a genie. His first wish is that his neighbor's cow should die. The genie asks the farmer, "What good will that do you?" "None," he replies with a smile of satisfaction, "but it will make my neighbor really unhappy." Simulations involving a quarrel over a fish catch that two businessmen want, one for the flesh of the fish and one for the skin, illustrate that not all problems have zero-sum outcomes. They also illustrate the importance of determining why a negotiator takes a particular position: a claim to the whole catch may conceal a need for only the fish skin. Underlying interests need to be discovered to be dealt with. Other simulations involved gaming in which communication and cooperative behavior are rewarded and "going it alone" is not.

Many topics were covered, but the focus of the lectures and exercises was on helping the participants make the key distinction between positions taken publicly or in negotiations and fundamental interests. The hope was to challenge them to think in terms of win-win solutions. This culminated on the last day with a participatory exercise in which the group collectively defined what they thought to be the Albanian position on Kosovo (independence now) as well as a score of interests underlying that position. Participants were then discomfited when asked to define the interests underlying the Serb position on Kosovo (maintain Serbian sovereignty). With initial difficulty but warming to the task, they developed a score of Serb interests. The overlap between some of the interests was quite apparent, and the group quickly understood that it was on the basis of these common interests that some sort of peace agreement might be built. The group anxiously packed up the butcher-block paper on which this exercise was conducted, only to have the police confiscate it at the Serbian border.

War intervened in the months after this event, killing one of the participants, Professor Bardhyl Caushi, and scattering many others as displaced people and refugees. Caushi was apparently murdered as Serb forces withdrew in June 1999, though his body was never found. Significantly older and more distinguished than the other participants, Caushi was a mild-mannered expert on constitutional law. His decision to remove his tie after two days of the workshop was considered a singular triumph. The other participants not only survived, but most have also thrived in the postwar period on the more democratically oriented side of Kosovo Albanian politics and civil society. Some of them view the workshop in Sofia as an important moment in their personal evolution, one that illustrated the virtue of remaining open to dialogue with adversaries. In addition to helping the participants improve their negotiating skills, the training appears to have encouraged political moderation, even under fairly extreme circumstances, at least among people already inclined in that direction.

The NATO-Yugoslavia war was over, but in June and July 1999 two new problems emerged. The expulsion of Serbs from Kosovo was not entirely unexpected because many had been employed in the Serbian administration. The ferocity of the expulsion was dramatic, however. In addition, violence began between Albanian factions, with apparent KLA attacks on LDK politicians and sympathizers. The KLA in fact took over municipal governance in much of Kosovo, which previously had been handled (outside official channels) by the LDK.

Both this violence against the Serbs and intra-Albanian violence inspired the planning of "Unity in Diversity: A Workshop on Democratic Coalition Building," which was hosted at the Lansdowne Conference Center in Virginia from September 10 through 14, 1999. Forty Kosovo Albanian political and civil society leaders were invited. Planning had in fact begun even before the end of the war. Bringing forty-two Kosovars to the United States for a week required resources far beyond those available from USIP's budget. When the war ended, the need for coalition building among the Albanians only grew. Financing for the event came from the State Department and assistance from the U.S. Office in Pristina, which chose the participants and

convinced them to come. Travel and translation—two enormously complicated administrative tasks—were handled by World Learning, working under a USAID contract and in cooperation with USIP.

The Lansdowne conference occurred at a delicate moment. The war was
still fresh in everyone's mind. Kosovo's future was not yet clear. It would become independent more than eight years later. In 1999, the Albanians were
sharply split between those who wanted to take credit for the military defeat
of the Serbs on the battlefield and those who emphasized the importance of
a decade of nonviolent resistance. The misunderstandings between these two
groups were in some ways as dramatic, and deadly, as disagreements with the
Serbs. Underneath lay the question of who would hold power in a Kosovo
that was free of Serb dominance.

The United States was an important point of reference for both groups.
USIP was a trusted broker, less familiar to the KLA participants than to
those who had participated in nonviolent resistance, but acceptable to both.
The two groups had in fact not developed a productive dialogue in Pristina.
They spent their days jockeying for position and undermining each other
rather than thinking hard about Kosovo's future or producing services for
its citizens.

The overall themes of the dialogue—that unity was possible in diversity
and that democracy would require coalition-building—were new to the participants. They were a Who's Who of politics and civil society in Kosovo at
the end of the war, with the notable exception of Ibrahim Rugova, who refused to come. They included the political leadership of the KLA and LDK
(minus Rugova) plus several other parties. But, significantly, they also included local political leaders, the major NGOs, independent thinkers, journalists, and economists. This was the first postwar exposure of the KLA to
civil society, and the clash was notable. In one memorable moment during a
facilitated discussion of the role of civil society in the "new" Kosovo, a newspaper editor challenged KLA leader Hashim Thaci's claim that he supported
press freedom by asking what Thaci would do if the newspaper published
a photograph of him naked. Thaci was reduced to speechlessness, but the
incident led on to a rich discussion of freedom of the press.

This interaction illustrates an important mechanism at work in Track 1.5
efforts such as this one. Left alone, politicians and government representatives will often continue their normal political sparring in a facilitated dialogue. The presence of civil society representatives breaks up the usual pattern and presents a serious challenge to business as usual. It also provides a
check on the politicians after they leave the event. It is sometimes said that

the Lansdowne event was a failure because the participants did not live up to the vision projected in the statement issued at the end of the meeting. In fact, the success of the meeting is clear in that, years later, the Lansdowne Declaration was still being used to measure performance. It is the NGO representatives, media people, and independent intellectuals who not only pressure politicians into constructive statements but also work to create accountability by using the statements as standards for assessing performance.

Most of the event time at Lansdowne was spent in three working groups: on the political process, on economic reconstruction, revitalization and reform, and on strengthening civil society. The division into working groups was not random. Each had some politicians, some economists, and some civil society people. This balance is difficult to achieve because politicians all want to be part of the "political" working group, economists part of the "economic" working group, and the civil society people part of the "civil society" working group. This seems logical enough, but leads to much less fruitful interaction. Political parties were therefore distributed as much as possible among the working groups to ensure a dynamic discussion. The division into working groups was prepared in the first instance by Ylber Bajraktari, a Kosovar Albanian refugee working for USIP. He proved invaluable throughout because he knew most of the participants, at least by reputation, and had an excellent feel for both them and USIP.

The task within the three working groups was the same: to project within each topic what kind of Kosovo the participants wanted to see in five years, to assess where Kosovo was at the moment, and to define what needed to be done to get to the desired future state. The approach keeps the focus on the future, especially important in this instance because all the peoples of the Balkans have an unfortunate tendency to bog themselves down in the past and to complain about the present without offering specific solutions. The future-oriented approach worked well under the guidance of the overall chairperson Dr. Chester Crocker (then chair of the USIP board of directors) and three experienced facilitators (George Ward, Hal Saunders, and Michael Froman), who intervened repeatedly to keep the discussion on track and prepared drafts of the report but were careful not to push specific ideas.

The report, known as the Lansdowne Declaration, went much further in defining Kosovo's bright future, difficult present, and practical steps in the right direction than we had imagined possible. Certainly the participants were in part telling USIP what they thought it wanted to hear. But for many this was a first opportunity to reflect in detail on what they really wanted. USIP has been told since that it was at Lansdowne that KLA leadership realized that it was now engaged in a political contest and would have to leave its military past behind. It seems clear that, although the KLA had already formally given up arms, the mental shift had not yet occurred when KLA leaders arrived at Lansdowne, and it is gratifying to think that the meeting may have had an impact on their thinking. Certainly intra-Albanian violence declined sharply after Lansdowne, though it continued at lowered levels for years after.

The Lansdowne meeting as a one-off event might have been useful, but that was not what USIP had in mind during planning. The event was seen as the beginning of an effort to get Albanians and Serbs talking to each other, though the Albanians would have regarded it as premature. So when Serbs complained vociferously about an event to discuss the future of Kosovo without them, USIP readily agreed to hold a similar event for them. The U.S. Office in Pristina again chose the participants, though the State Department provided no funding. The workshop "Options for Building Multiethnic and Democratic Institutions in Kosovo" was convened in Sofia, Bulgaria, from December 10 to 12, 1999, under the chairmanship of Landrum Bolling, whose many virtues include the fact that he was present at the liberation of Sarajevo in 1944.

Again the aim was to include both politicians and nonpoliticians, but the range was limited in several ways. First, there was not much left of Serbian civil society in Kosovo in December 1999—no media, few professors (the Serbian university of Pristina had been evacuated to Serbia), and few NGOs. The mainstay of Serbian civil society at that point was the Orthodox Church, which attended in the person of Bishop Artemije (his assistant, the monk Sava, had been in on the planning but was ill and could not attend). A number of local leaders came, all associated with the Serb National Council led by the bishop, prominent among them the Albanian-speaking Josif Vasic, who was later murdered in Gnjilane/Gjilan. At the bishop's request, three participants came from Belgrade. The Center for Liberal Studies, a democratically oriented Bulgarian think tank, provided logistical and administrative support.

The Serbs arrived grumbling and suspicious. One prominent politician said that he had come only because the bishop had insisted. Milosevic was still in power in Belgrade, and several no doubt felt politically exposed being at a meeting hosted by USIP, which by then was well known for having prepared a plan for providing U.S. support to democratic forces in Serbia. It took a concerted effort to overcome the resistance and gain the confidence of the participants. Landrum Bolling deserves a good deal of credit for his account of how he obtained Tito's personal permission to attend the liberation of Sarajevo, as did David Steele, then with the Center for Strategic and International Studies (CSIS), who worked as one of the facilitators. The bishop played a critical role—he wanted a statement from a unified Serb group that would match the Lansdowne Declaration of the Albanians and prepare the way for talks.

The Sofia Declaration that emerged from the two working groups, one on politics and one on humanitarian issues and refugee return, established the position of the Serbs on most of the major issues. Discussions followed the previous pattern: project a desirable future five years out, describe the current situation, and define steps in the right direction. One of the Belgrade participants, historian Dusan Batakovic (later ambassador in Athens, Ottawa, and Paris), had before the war put forward proposals to "cantonalize" Kosovo, creating some majority Serb cantons in rural areas. He pursued this proposal at Sofia, focusing on the remaining Serb enclaves, but found the bishop resistant. Territorial division of any sort would not satisfy the church's need to be present throughout Kosovo. The Serbs opted instead for decentralization and strong local self-government, ideas that they pursued for a decade thereafter. Although their unity did not last, the Sofia Declaration satisfied the Serbs' need to speak out and to match the Albanian vision for Kosovo.

Community-Level Dialogue

A meeting that included both Serbs and Albanians was next on the agenda, but facilitation first took what turned out to be a happy detour. It had become apparent soon after the Lansdowne meeting that participants were not taking prompt action to fulfill the promises made in the declaration. Hoping to preserve at least the spirit of Lansdowne, USIP asked the chief of the U.S. Office in Pristina, Lawrence Rossin, whether any local groups of Serbs and Albanians were prepared to deal with each other on a practical plane. Convinced that stability in post-conflict situations must be built from the bottom up, USIP was prepared to offer conflict management training to such a group, if it existed. Rossin in turn passed on the question to the U.S. commanding general of Task Force Falcon at Camp Bondsteel, who canvassed his units throughout the American area of responsibility.

Shortly after the Sofia meeting, the executive officer of one of the battalions located at Camp Monteith, the U.S. base located just outside the center of Gnjilane/Gjilan, said that his unit had been working with such a group for some time. It turned out that in the immediate aftermath of the war in Kosovo, five local civic leaders, three Albanians and two Serbs, had begun meeting secretly with the aim of restoring some of the interethnic cooperative endeavors that had existed before the conflict. Serbs and Albanians in the Gnjilane area have historically maintained relatively good relations. However, in the war's aftermath, violence against Serbs, including many killings, was rife. Merely by meeting together, the members of the small group were risking their lives.

Interestingly, the Gnjilane group had already heard of the Lansdowne meeting and even begun to call themselves the Lansdowne Group. By the beginning of 2000, the group felt that it had built the foundation for a dialogue that merited expansion. Through the U.S. Army, the group asked USIP to offer a workshop on coexistence in a multiethnic society to a group of nineteen Albanians and fourteen Serbs selected by the core Lansdowne Group. Because communication with the army so far had been only by email, it was essential at this point to visit Camp Monteith in person. The trip confirmed not only that an armored Humvee is one of the most uncomfortable ways to travel yet invented, but also that the army had the means and the will to organize a workshop on the base that would be conducted simultaneously in English, Serbian, and Albanian.

The workshop took place from May 3 through 6, 2000. The setting was a former Yugoslav Army headquarters building, now used for the same purpose by the U.S. Army. In one of the rooms used for the workshop, a portrait of Josef Broz Tito looked down sternly on the participants. The portrait had been "liberated" during the hostilities by a soldier, but later returned to its former place. All participants seemed to enjoy its presence. The venue was spartan but functional. The army provided a group of wonderfully enthusiastic and committed, albeit inexperienced, interpreters. The mission of the Organization for Security and Co-operation (OSCE) in Europe did its part by furnishing the only functional set of simultaneous interpretation gear in Kosovo. On the morning of May 3, the group gathered in the chilly lobby of the headquarters building. The Serbs arrived, for their own protection, in armored Humvees. Small mono-ethnic groups of Serbs and Albanians gathered, casting furtive glances at one another. Most had known each other for years, though since separated by the war.

The facilitation team consisted of Dr. David Steele of CSIS, Dr. Lewis Rasmussen, then with USIP, and authors Dan Serwer and George Ward. The program focused on three objectives—establishing dialogue, acquiring conflict management skills, and solving concrete problems. The first was clearly the most essential. Participants were separated into groups of seven or eight and asked to relate their firsthand experiences during the conflict.

The accounts were often dramatic and moving. They helped the participants, who included both KLA fighters and former police and Yugoslav Army soldiers, realize that everyone had suffered in some measure, and that issues often portrayed in black-and-white terms were in fact composed of shades of gray. These narratives, especially those that contained vignettes of Serbs helping Albanians during the conflict or Albanians helping Serbs live through the post-conflict period, broke the ice. Friendships were not re-established, but working relationships were. The results of the concluding problem-solving working groups were a series of concrete work plans on issues of politics, economics, and education.

The progress toward dialogue fueled additional interethnic cooperation. Under the leadership of the core Lansdowne Group, civic leaders in Gnjilane, with the support of the U.S. Army and the U.S. Office in Pristina, decided that it might be possible to institutionalize interethnic cooperation by establishing a nongovernmental organization. The NGO they envisioned would be called the Council of Professionals, and would include sections for the various professions—physicians, educators, agricultural engineers, infrastructure experts, and so on. The U.S. Army agreed to furnish an office and physical security; the U.S. Office in Pristina provided a financial grant to cover start-up and initial operating costs. The remaining tasks were fleshing out the vision for the organization and gaining the active support of a larger group of civic and political leaders.

Again, the Lansdowne Group turned to USIP, this time for a workshop aimed at helping the group mold a cohesive, interethnic team for the NGO and formulate a work program. In April 2001, George Ward, David Steele, Robert Schoenhaus, and Rebecca Kilhefner, a USIP contractor with extensive experience in Kosovo, returned to Camp Monteith. The U.S. Army staff there had completely turned over from the previous year but offered the same outstanding support and cooperation.

The thirty-three participants who attended, eleven Serbs and twenty-two Albanians, were far more relaxed with each other than the previous year, at least in part because the level of interethnic violence had fallen in the meantime to virtually zero. Although recitations of old grievances were sometimes heard during the workshop, the participants focused readily on developing their negotiation and organizational skills and on agreeing on a detailed list of objectives for the Council of Professionals. Most striking in comparison to the previous year was the spirited participation of Serbs in the debate.

At the closing ceremony of the workshop, the collegial atmosphere reflected the group's determination to move forward toward cooperation on professional concerns. The five founders of the Lansdowne Group revealed their identities to the larger group and gave an account of their initial, clandestine dialogues. The Council of Professionals was well launched. In subsequent months, it succeeded in promoting several concrete interethnic initiatives, including cooperation between Serb and Albanian physicians to provide service at the local hospital, joint purchase of seeds for farmers, and joint proposal of a project for irrigation of farmlands. It continued to be active for years.

Multiethnic Programs

Soon after the first workshop in Gnjilane in July 2000, the U.S. Office in Pristina and the Department of State signed on to a USIP proposal to facilitate a discussion among a broad spectrum of Kosovar Albanian and Serb community leaders about how to build and maintain coexistence in a multiethnic society. The workshop was intended to identify issues for productive engagement and develop an agenda for cooperation. The event, held at Airlie House near Warrenton, Virginia, included twenty-seven Albanian and fourteen Serb participants. The USIP team was led by board chair Chester Crocker and included board member (later National Security Adviser) Stephen Hadley, executive vice president Harriet Hentges, and authors Dan Serwer and George Ward. Simultaneous interpretation was provided not only for the plenary sessions but also for the two problem-solving working groups in which participants spent most of their time.

The facilitators' hope was that the participants at Airlie House would chart a course for converting the bold words of the Lansdowne and Sofia Declarations into real accomplishments on the ground. Discussions were spirited and often stormy. In Gnjilane, the storytelling portion of the program had been useful in working through some of the emotions that lay so close to the surface. At Airlie, formal storytelling was omitted under the assumption that the participants were past needing it. This was not the case. As one working group was striving to reach closure on a series of important issues, an Albanian participant burst out with a tearful account of the murder of her husband and sons by Serb paramilitary police. She accused one of the Serb participants of being complicit in the murders. Naturally, proceedings stopped dead and resumed only after a considerable effort by the facilitator. Had a period been set aside earlier for a storytelling session and personal narratives, time likely would have been saved in the end.

At key intervals during the discussions, the chair played a pivotal role. Crocker and Hadley displayed both empathy and toughness in helping participants work through disagreements that might have caused the meeting to end in rancor. They facilitated a session among the most senior participants that produced the preamble for what became the Airlie Declaration. This document accentuated the positive, problem-solving character of the meeting, but made clear that the wounds of the past were "so fresh and so deep that they make it more difficult to proceed without more time for healing."

In the end, helpful, concrete agreements at Airlie proved possible. The most important was the launch of an initiative, the Campaign Against Violence, to promote tolerance, condemn violence, prevent negative exploitation of ethnic issues, and enable physical integration and political participation by all. The participants agreed, among other things, to participate in a public Day Against Violence, to promote the campaign by personal appearances, to establish multiethnic dialogues at the local level, and to launch a media campaign in support of the initiative.

As noted, the value of the earlier Lansdowne Declaration had been diminished by the lack of follow-through in Kosovo. Trying to ensure that the Airlie statement did not suffer the same fate, the USIP facilitators resolved to hold the participants to their words. USIP dispatched American consultants to Kosovo to work with the Airlie participants. At Airlie, all of the participants had been presented with Internet-ready laptop computers, donated by the Waitt Foundation. One consultant established arrangements for email communications among participants. Another shuttled tirelessly between Albanian and Serb communities to put in place arrangements for the Day Against Violence. In the end, the initiative was a success, as were a series of joint visits by Albanian and Serb political leaders to key localities.

Efforts to create a continuing electronic dialogue among the Airlie participants did not succeed, however. Despite many technical difficulties in war-ravaged Kosovo, we were able to get almost everyone on line through extensive technical assistance by contracted "e-riders." Many of the participants used their computers for email communications—in one case to contact a U.S. senator. But cyberspace proved not safe enough for continuation of the interethnic dialogue begun at Airlie. USIP would have had to invest heavily in providing content, something deemed both inconsistent with the overall objectives and excessively costly.

Facilitation as Training

Beginning with municipal elections in October 2000, the democratic transition in Kosovo moved into a new phase. The U.S. Department of State and the U.S. Office in Pristina continued to provide both moral and financial support to USIP's facilitation efforts. The United Nations administrator for Kosovo and the chief of mission of the OSCE also showed active interest in USIP's efforts. Their input was key to the next stage of the facilitation, which involved two additional gatherings at Airlie House.

Training workshops in conflict management and resolution are often appropriately seen as forms of third-party intervention in conflicts. The next steps taken by USIP—organizing two training workshops—were planned with that principle in mind. In February 2001, the State Department sponsored a visit to the United States of forty-four newly elected mayors, deputy mayors, and municipal council members from Kosovo. Following the Kosovo-wide elections in November 2001, a similar visit was arranged for thirty members of the Kosovo Assembly in June 2002. At the request of the State Department, USIP offered both groups four-day training workshops that focused on building skills for coexistence, effective management, and good governance. These workshops included not only Albanian Kosovars and Serbs but also leaders from the other ethnic groups in Kosovo, such as Roma, Turks, Ashkali, and Bosniacs.

In each case, the workshops included components similar to those used at the Gnjilane events—participant narratives, assessment of personal conflict styles, practice in negotiation skills, a simulation with a scenario appropriate for the group's governing responsibilities, and problem-solving working groups. Both workshops resulted in agreement on additional concrete steps toward peaceful coexistence. At the municipal workshop, the participants agreed to form a multiethnic, Kosovo-wide association of municipal officials, which would become a vehicle for receiving constituent views and building professional expertise in the field of public administration. This was an important success, though tragically, in October 2002, one of the leading proponents of the association, Uke Bytyci, was murdered in a politically motivated attack. Assembly members agreed on an initial agenda and on arrangements for ensuring that the government heard the views of civic groups and NGOs. But their performance immediately following the meeting—in Washington as well as after their return to Kosovo—was contentious. This might have been due in part to the presence of only politicians. There were no civil society leaders to keep them to their pledges or moderate their stances.

USIP also pursued interethnic dialogue beyond Kosovo's borders. Beginning in 1998, Albert Cevallos, a USIP consultant, had been working in Serbia with groups opposed to the rule of President Milosevic. Soon after Milosevic's fall, Cevallos conceived of a program to promote dialogue among young Serbian leaders from Yugoslavia and young Albanian leaders in Kosovo. This program, named Partnerships for Peace, began with a small meeting in Montenegro in July 2001. A larger gathering followed in Vienna in October of the same year. The Vienna meeting included thirty of the most prominent young civic and political leaders of Kosovo and Serbia. The program eventually grew to include more than 120 participants.

In September 2002, with funding from the U.S. Agency for International Development, USIP brought thirty members of this group to Washington for an intensive one-week program in team building and problem-solving. The vehicles chosen were unusual for the Balkans context. Ice was broken with a "ropes" course in suburban Virginia that presented interesting mental and physical challenges as well as an opportunity for the young leaders to see the more mature facilitators in a highly informal setting. A daylong course in negotiation and mediation skills followed. The group then participated in a three-day, complex simulation—developed by the Institute for Defense Analyses with USIP participation—involving an economy and society in transition from war to democratic, free-market institutions. Some twenty U.S. officials responsible for the Balkans, academics, and NGO representatives also participated. The simulation, which involved a computer-based model of a fictitious post-conflict society, placed participants under significant pressure as they worked through ten years of policy and business decisions in the short game period. The participants found the simulation exhilarating and an excellent team-building vehicle. The experience they gained working together on simulated problems helped them agree to undertake jointly on their return to the Balkans a series of activities aimed at improving interethnic relations. They agreed, for example, to cooperate in urging minority voters to go to the polls in upcoming elections, and they pledged to help relieve the isolation of ethnic enclaves through a program of visits and exchanges.

Efforts on Kosovo and Serbia continued for several more years, and included conflict management training for upwards of 20 percent of the officers in the Serbian Foreign Ministry and preparation of the provisional institutions of self-government in Kosovo for talks with Belgrade, which did not actually begin until 2011.

Assessment

Any serious evaluation of efforts to facilitate dialogue must avoid confusing outputs with outcomes. In this case, the outputs of USIP's efforts were nine or ten facilitated dialogues and training workshops conducted over approximately three years that engaged Serbs and Albanian Kosovars in discussions about interethnic coexistence and coalition building. But what were the outcomes? What did these many hours of work around tables actually accomplish?

First, they reacquainted key people from both sides with one another and helped them reinitiate practical cooperation. The degree of personal estrangement produced by ethnic conflict is difficult to overstate. In the absence of dialogue, individual narratives of conflict within each ethnic group tend to magnify and feed off each other, producing ultimately a highly sectarian amalgam that is antithetical to dialogue. As demonstrated in Gnjilane, men and women who had known each other for decades would not even look each other in the face at the outset. After months of working together in facilitated dialogues, they were able not only to agree on practical measures in their mutual interests, but also to engage in constructive, civil discourse.

Second, the facilitated dialogues produced a series of documents that, taken together, serve as de facto standards for interethnic cooperation, dialogue, good governance, and economic and social reform in Kosovo. Oddly enough, this is true even though none of the documents have any official standing. At most, as at Lansdowne, they were agreed on by participants acting in their individual capacities. In other instances, as at the 2002 program for members of the Kosovo Assembly, the facilitators produced and took responsibility for the documents. Despite these circumstances, on countless occasions the resultant documents have been held up as standards to which representatives of all ethnic groups should adhere.

Third, the dialogues reinforced and built on each other. Without the Lansdowne Declaration, the five courageous civic leaders in Kosovo would probably never have felt empowered to expand and intensify their dialogue and turn it into a program of action. Without the first encounter between Serbs and Albanians at Airlie, it would have been difficult or even impossible to formulate the terms of reference for the subsequent practical forums for municipal officials and legislators. Without the mono-ethnic programs for Serb and Albanian leaders, neither group would have felt itself cohesive or self-confident enough to engage the other.

Fourth, the dialogues filled communications gaps that could not be covered through official arrangements. For example, despite having served together in the Kosovo Assembly for more than six months by the time they arrived at Airlie in June 2002, hardly any of the participants, whether Serb or Albanian, personally knew individuals from the other side. During exercises, simulations, coffee breaks, and late-evening sessions in the lounge, people became acquainted on a personal level. They left Airlie able to converse with each other and even, in some cases, to laugh together.

Fifth, the dialogues opened communications between political leaders and representatives of civil society. At Lansdowne, political leaders were clearly uncomfortable with the fact that the facilitators included NGO leaders in the political working group. For the first time, politicians were forced to listen to the opinions and views of nonparty civic activists. They sometimes clearly did not enjoy the experience, but they listened—both at Lansdowne and when they returned to Kosovo.

Sixth, the dialogues were an opportunity for representatives of the U.S. government and international organizations to interact with leaders from Kosovo on an unofficial, not-for-attribution basis. Conversely, the occasions gave the leaders of Kosovo an opportunity to see the human side of the international presence. Because of the legal role played by the international authority in Kosovo, decisions by the UN administrator were often controversial. The U.S. government, UN, and OSCE observers at the workshops and dialogues played an invaluable role by providing background and context to the decisions of the international community on Kosovo.

Seventh, the dialogues resulted in concrete agreements that have made Kosovo a safer, more peaceful place and have brightened its future prospects. In the Gnjilane region, the dialogue efforts helped reduce interethnic violence and caused a U.S. commander to say that the lives of some American soldiers had likely been saved. The first Airlie meeting resulted in a campaign against violence that demonstrated to people on the street that progress was possible. The mayors agreed on a permanent unofficial forum for municipal officials. The assembly members were able to map out an agenda for their work. Finally, the young leaders from Serbia and Kosovo began a series of practical steps to relieve the isolation of Serbian enclaves in Kosovo and Albanian populations in Serbia.

Lessons Learned

• *Choosing the right team is essential.*
Core facilitators need the assistance of experts and specialists. Landrum Bolling brought with him to Sofia a high degree of credibility with leaders of the Orthodox faith. David Steele, who worked in the dialogues in Gnjilane and at Airlie, had a special ability to relate intercommunal conflicts to personal needs and fears. Hal Saunders and Michael Froman brought special expertise in dealing with civil society organizations and economic transi-

tion, respectively, to the work at Lansdowne. A robust support team is also necessary. The meetings at Camp Monteith required the assistance of up to 100 soldiers, who provided secure transport for Serb participants, escorted participants on base, assisted in facilitation, and prepared meals. Capable and motivated interpreters are also critical. In Gnjilane, a motivated team of young interpreters made up with enthusiasm for the limitations of an inadequate electronic system and their own lack of training in simultaneous interpretation. On the other side of the coin, an interpreter who could not put aside her own political views materially impeded progress at the first Airlie meeting. In addition to interpreters, the USIP team usually includes a native speaker of whatever languages are to be used, preferably one who knows the participants (at least by reputation) and who is familiar enough with USIP to credibly raise a red flag on any impending problems.

• *First impressions are important.*

As demonstrated in Sofia, it is extremely important that the facilitators make it clear that they regard the participants as people whose comfort and convenience should be served, within reasonable limits. Visible signals of respect are important. This is not to suggest that deluxe arrangements must be made. Such would be impossible in any case in many zones of conflict. When reasonably comfortable and safe facilities cannot be arranged within the zone of conflict, however, facilitators should consider transferring the participants to a safer venue. Reasonably comfortable travel arrangements are critical: the first Airlie workshop started with grumpy Albanians due to bad flight connections.·

• *Focus on the future.*

Visitors to the Balkans are familiar with the tendency of the inhabitants to relate present circumstances to events of the past. Events that are seen as pivotal, such as the Battle of Kosovo Polje in 1389, are dwelt on to excess, and lines of causality are drawn from the past to the present. This process does little to increase understanding of the past and much to deepen ethnic hostilities of the present. It is an obstacle in the way of effective dialogues for peace. As David Steele said during his presentation to the Lansdowne group in Gnjilane, "Forgiveness means giving up all hope of a better past." One effective way to avoid focusing on the past is to begin the facilitation process by asking participants to describe in detail the sort of future to which they aspire. The facilitator should then ask the participants to describe the present in terms of the same categories. The third and final step involves coaching the participants to describe the paths critical to the transition. This technique proved consistently productive in all of the facilitated dialogues under consideration. A principal challenge for the facilitator using this technique is to gently but firmly prohibit participants from dwelling on the problems of the past.

- *Unilateral preparation should come before multilateral progress.*
In situations involving deeply rooted ethnic conflict, divisions within each group are often almost as severe as those between groups. In the case of Kosovo, the principal fissure within the Albanian community was between the nonviolent approach advocated by Ibrahim Rugova and his Democratic League of Kosovo and the political descendants of the violent Kosovo Liberation Army, led by Hashim Thaci and others. Likewise, the Serb community was divided between those, including Bishop Artemije, at the time inclined toward accommodation with the Albanian majority and more intransigent figures loyal to the regime in Belgrade. Had the facilitated dialogue begun in a bi-ethnic setting, the process would have been disrupted and probably undone by tensions within each group. Through separate facilitated dialogues with Serbs and Albanians, each group was able to identify its core interests and to distinguish those interests from the political positions and postures that they had assumed. This process meant that bi-ethnic discussions, once begun, could proceed relatively rapidly.

- *Dialogue should be multilevel.*
After Lansdowne, the interethnic dialogue seemed to stall at the Pristina level. The progress made in Gnjilane then provided an illustration that permanent deadlock was not inevitable. The mayor of Gnjilane initiated the proposal for a national association of municipal leaders. Thus, just as the leaders in Gnjilane received their inspiration from the words of the Lansdowne Declaration, the process begun at Lansdowne was able to move forward on the basis of concrete progress made in Gnjilane.

- *Politics are too important to leave to the politicians.*
Relatively small working groups were the primary forums during the Kosovo workshops. In preparing for the Lansdowne meeting, the decision was made to ensure an even mixture of participants from all backgrounds in each working group. Thus, NGO leaders, economists, civic leaders, journalists, professional people—and politicians—populated the political working group. Economists were a minority in the economics working group. This formula

was not popular, but virtually all of the sometimes vociferous demands for reassignment to another working group were resisted. In the end, this proved one of the best decisions made in organizing the facilitation. Nonpoliticians held the politicians accountable in the political working group. The same was true for noneconomists in the economics working group.

• *Let people tell their stories.*
The sad incident has already been related in which, during a working session, a woman angrily confronted a person whom she believed complicit in the murders of her husband and sons. That workshop had offered no structured opportunity for participants to relate their first-person narratives of the conflict. Other workshops did, enabling facilitators to channel the very understandable and justifiable anger that emerged into more constructive directions. Storytelling sessions were challenging in any case. It was often necessary to remind participants to refrain from second- and third-party narratives, and to stay within the envelope of their personal knowledge.

• *Dialogues need to be connected by actions.*
When, after Lansdowne, participants failed to live up to the words of the declaration they had just signed, the facilitation project seemed threatened. In Gnjilane, the U.S. Army provided valuable, day-by-day monitoring of the implementation of workshop undertakings. After the first Airlie meeting, USIP consultants in the field performed a monitoring function. With the increasing engagement in the process of the U.S. Office in Pristina, the UN, and the OSCE, those entities also helped greatly in follow-up efforts.

• *The facilitator's lot is not (always) a happy one.*
Some would argue that facilitators should stay neutral in the discussions and focus exclusively on the process, but that was not how they behaved in this series of dialogues. A facilitator should ordinarily not put personal proposals on the table, but will often need to rephrase or even reshape ideas that others introduce. Many of these discussions, for example, would not have progressed as far as they did had the facilitators been unwilling or unable to contribute substantively, yet respect the integrity of the participants' contributions and always ensure that the participants in the end felt they "owned" the results. He or she must be committed to the process and at least relatively expert in the problems at hand. These requirements demand a great deal of sustained intellectual effort and physical and emotional stamina. The facilitator must concentrate full time and attention on the substance of dis-

cussions. It is extremely important to ensure that each facilitator is provided with assistants to attend to taking notes, helping with flip charts, and taking care of logistical requirements.

Despite these challenges, we should not lose sight of the reality that conducting facilitated dialogues among parties in conflict can be immensely rewarding and productive. The process is intense and fast-moving. Dialogue yields learning about culture and context that cannot be gleaned from textbooks and monographs. Enduring connections and friendships can develop. Few professional experiences are more rewarding than when, as in this case, a dialogue results in measurable and lasting progress toward peaceful management of a conflict. To paraphrase the childhood aphorism, "Sticks and stones can break bones, but words can start the healing."

4

Religion: Inter- and Intrafaith Dialogue
Susan Hayward and Lucy Kurtzer-Ellenbogen

Religion is typically considered a taboo subject by polite visitors to conflict zones. After all, it conjures strong feelings. Many fear they will say the wrong thing and cause offense. But it is for just such sensitive subjects that facilitated dialogue—conversation between conflicting parties that is facilitated by a neutral third party—can be useful. The Religion and Peacemaking Program at USIP uses facilitated inter- and intrafaith dialogue (IFD) as an essential component of its work in conflict zones, particularly in places where religion is a driver of the conflict. This chapter takes two projects, both supported by USIP, as case studies through which to examine religious dialogue, sketch the shape and scope it can take, depending on the objectives and the participants, and highlight some of the challenges those wishing to launch it must bear in mind.

Background

What constitutes inter- and intrafaith dialogue? How does it relate to and differ from secular facilitated dialogue? IFD is a subsector within the larger field of facilitated dialogue, one that expressly engages religion with respect to either the content of discussion or the identity of the participants. The goals are similar to those of other secular dialogue projects: to gain mutual understanding, strengthen positive relationships, and create avenues to find solutions to shared problems. IFD, however, often has concurrent goals that relate to its religious character. These may include challenging destructive religious stereotyping and bias, understanding the religious practices and beliefs of others, and increasing the capacity and willingness of religious leaders to pursue peacebuilding work. Elsewhere, Susan Hayward has described IFD this way:

> The goal is not to convert, to assert the superiority of one faith, or to conflate different religions by diluting them into one common denominator, but to appreciate similarities and differences between religions. Moreover, participants often come to understand how one's faith shapes one's position on particular issues pertinent in their context. As such, participants use the framework of religion not only to build relationships, but also, often, as doorways into discussions about central social and political concerns driving inter-communal conflict.[1]

IFD facilitated effectively over a sustained period engenders a level of trust that moves participants beyond superficial engagement to a level at which they honestly reflect on and struggle together over sensitive and provocative issues. This kind of honest, engaged dialogue helps create peaceful coexistence between religious communities, often cited as a requisite for sustainable peace. In and outside conflict zones, peaceful religious coexistence goes beyond mere religious tolerance or the adoption of legal protections for religious freedom. It develops in environments in which diverse religions live together with mutual respect and open engagement. IFD fosters such environments by creating opportunities for face-to-face contact and deep relationship building. The goal is not for participants to agree with one another on every social, political, economic, or theological issue but instead to understand and appreciate other viewpoints, and to find places of shared agreement for collective action. Most important is that participants are committed to living peaceably together by addressing conflict nonviolently when it arises between them, and to developing rights-respecting policies and attitudes that do not infringe on the worldview and practices of other communities. These dialogue sessions ideally help eradicate negative stereotyping and bias among the participants, and in turn enable the participants to recognize and confront negative stereotypes and bias in their communities.

IFD can be particularly useful in places where religion is driving violence. Once a significant level of trust is established among participants, IFD can be used to explore honestly teachings that are driving violence or bias, to consider them alongside other teachings in the tradition, and to understand the effects of particular interpretations on other communities. For example, scholar and former USIP Jennings Randolph Senior Fellow Mohammed

---

1. Susan Hayward, "Peace through Inter and Intra Religious Dialogue," presentation at the International Symposium on Religions and World Peace, Osnabrueck, Germany, October 23, 2010, 5.

Abu-Nimer has written about how interfaith dialogue in Israel-Palestine has led participants to consider particular teachings about "chosen people" or jihad, and how they play out in that context. This, in turn, has helped participants critically evaluate their own traditions.[2]

Finally, IFD can promote attitudinal changes. Through the dialogue process, participants gain new information and hear new perspectives, and often, as a result, their understanding changes. After experiencing a constructive encounter with someone from a different community against whom one previously felt fear or bias, one's emotional response to the other community often changes. The religious nature of the dialogues can amplify this attitudinal shift. After all, when one discusses one's faith, spiritual experiences, and religious beliefs, one is likely to speak from a deeply rooted place within oneself. Engaging at this level, personal transformation is more likely to result, and so commitments to pursuing social justice and peacebuilding activities may be more energetically held.

IFD can engage participants from a variety of strata within society, from the grassroots level up through the senior religious, academic, or political leadership within a community. At each of these levels, the dialogue's objectives and processes must be altered to fit the needs and interests of the participants. IFD can be conducted as a one-off event but, to have lasting impact, it is best as a sustained series. Participants should be encouraged to commit for a long period of regular engagement from the beginning of the process. Topics can vary from theological issues such as the afterlife or the nature of God or truth, to general social and political issues, or to pertinent shared global problems.

It is one thing to talk generally about IFD, and another to dive into the details, where the real lessons emerge. In what follows, we offer two case studies to explore IFD in action. The first is the Alexandria process in Israel-Palestine, which was initiated by senior Christian, Jewish, and Muslim religious leaders. Together, members of this group, all of whom were male and some of whom also served in political roles, sought to lend interfaith support to the political track of the Middle East peace process by forging a cooperative and religiously grounded approach to stemming the violence afflicting the region. The Colombian initiative, by contrast, involves middle-range and lower-level religious women (only some of whom are traditional ordained leaders—pastors and nuns) whose dialogue has focused on

2. Mohammed Abu-Nimer, "The Miracles of Transformation through Interfaith Dialogue," in *Interfaith Dialogue and Peacemaking*, edited by David Smock (Washington, DC: U.S. Institute of Peace Press, 2002), 23.

sharing personal experience, local manifestations of conflict, and initiatives for peacebuilding within their local communities. Both of these experiences surface lessons about how to implement IFD effectively and sensitively. Juxtaposed, these studies shed light on the value and limitations inherent in different approaches to IFD.

The Alexandria Process

In 2000, key Israeli and Palestinian Jewish, Muslim, and Christian leaders, frustrated with the failure of the peace process and new waves of violence, decided that the time had come to lead a distinctively religious approach to peace. Their initial meetings culminated with an interfaith summit in late January 2002 in Alexandria, Egypt. There, Israeli, Palestinian, and Egyptian leaders from the three major monotheistic faiths discussed ways to jointly end the violence that was consuming the lives of those in the region. The result was the First Alexandria Declaration of the Religious Leaders of the Holy Land. The document contained a condemnation of ongoing violence, a commitment to work jointly for peace in mutual respect for each other's faith and connection to the land, and a call for the resumption and implementation of the stalled political peace process.[3]

Dating the conflict that is the subject of the Alexandria process has always been difficult. The sheer variety of nomenclatures given to it—the Middle East conflict, the Arab-Israeli conflict, the Israeli-Palestinian conflict, or the Jewish-Arab conflict—hints at the difficulty of neatly defining its historical, geographic, or even ideological parameters. Like many conflicts defined as religious in nature, the one being waged primarily between Israelis and Palestinians is arguably first a conflict over resources, in this case, land. However, given the religiously charged nature of that territory, religious discourse, symbols, and identities have been invoked in defense of territorial claims. Therefore, although some Christians, Jews, and Muslims alike will draw on their sacred texts to substantiate their positions on the dynamics of the conflict, it is also possible to date the roots of the violence to the late nineteenth century.

At that time, against the backdrop of a waning Ottoman Empire, adherents of Arab nationalism and of its Jewish counterpart, Zionism, found themselves competing for the same piece of real estate in what was then

---

3. For the full text, see "The First Alexandria Declaration of the Religious Leaders of the Holy Land," Israeli Ministry of Foreign Affairs, January 21, 2001, http://www.mfa.gov.il/MFA/MFAArchive/2000_2009/2002/1/.

Ottoman-controlled Palestine. The Zionist movement promoted a return of Jews to their ancestral homeland of Israel and the eventual establishment of a Jewish state there. Fueled by rampant anti-Semitism across Europe, the movement grew in strength during the early decades of the twentieth century, which were marked by increased Jewish migration to Palestine and by a series of violent clashes between Arab and Jewish inhabitants of the land. After Britain gained mandatory power of the area in 1922, it soon lost the ability to deal with the violent reactions that ensued. At the end of World War II, with waves of Holocaust survivors looking for a home, Britain referred the matter to the United Nations (UN), which in 1947 adopted a partition plan for Palestine, calling for the division of the territory into an Arab state, a Jewish state, and a UN-controlled *corpus separatum* around Jerusalem. The Arabs in Palestine and the Arab League rejected this plan. Tensions escalated as Jewish and Arab communities in Palestine became enmeshed in a cycle of violent and fatal attacks, reprisals, and counterreprisals. When the British mandate expired in May 1948 and the Jewish leadership in Palestine declared the creation of the State of Israel, Arab forces attacked. The nascent Israeli Defense Forces were victorious, pushing the borders beyond those originally prescribed by the UN partition plan and, in the process, creating several hundred thousand Palestinian refugees. Israelis, Palestinians, and Arabs from neighboring states have since suffered the violent and fatal consequences of six more wars waged between Israel and its Arab neighbors,[4] two major Palestinian uprisings (intifadas), and waves of terrorist attacks and reprisals.

Through this long-lived and ongoing cycle of competing claims, dueling narratives, and mutually destructive violence, a series of diplomatic attempts have failed to bring about a peaceful, enduring, and mutually agreeable resolution. Collectively, these attempts have come to be known as the Middle East peace process. This process entered a new phase in the 1990s with the signing of the Oslo Accords, the first face-to-face agreement between the Israeli government and the Palestinians that included the conditions considered necessary for a future Palestinian state. However, by 2000 the peace process lay moribund. The 1995 assassination of Israel's prime minister by a right-wing religious Jew who opposed the peace process and a wave of suicide bombings targeting Israeli civilians carried out by Islamist groups had

---

4. The Suez Crisis of 1956, which pitted Israel, along with Britain and France, against Egypt; the 1967 Six-Day War, which saw Israel in combat with Egypt, Jordan, and Syria; the 1973 war between Israel and an Arab coalition led by Egypt and Syria; the 1982 war between Israel and Lebanon; a second Israel-Lebanon war in 2006; and Operation Cast Lead, or the Gaza War of 2008, in which Israel attacked Hamas-controlled Gaza in response to rocket fire into southern Israel.

effectively stopped all progress in its tracks. When in 2000 an attempt by U.S. President Bill Clinton to get the Oslo process back on track failed,[5] faith on both sides broke down and within two months, what became known as the second intifada had erupted, exacting a high cost on both sides in terms of lives destroyed and lost.

It was against this backdrop in January 2002—when the violence of the second intifada was at its apex—that Jewish, Muslim, and Christian leaders met in Alexandria to "pray for true peace in Jerusalem and the Holy Land, and declare our commitment to ending the violence and bloodshed that denies the right of life and dignity."[6]

The Process

Writing about the Alexandria Declaration, Yehezkel Landau observed that it was a conviction of those religious leaders who brought about the process that "the Oslo process failed, in part, because it was a secular peace plan imposed by secular leaders on a Holy Land, where large and influential minorities of both Jews and Palestinians are motivated by deeply held religious convictions."[7] The idea was not to replace secular channels of diplomacy but instead to complement them. This was an acknowledgment that in a conflict region of utmost religious significance to three groups, a religious approach to reconciliation was necessary. The goal was to find agreement on promoting peace and opposing violence in terms that resonated equally among those involved. A key initiator of the process was Rabbi Michael Melchior, who at the time of the summit was serving as deputy minister of foreign affairs in Prime Minister Ariel Sharon's government. Melchior lamented that the pursuers of the peace process had closed the door to engagement in matters of faith and religion and, in so doing, had given primacy to radical religious forces, who were acting as spoilers. In a conversation with Melchior eight years on from Alexandria, he reiterated this belief, adding that because of the secular nature of the peace process and those driving it, the very notion of peace in Israeli society had become, and continues to be, identified with the secular left. Therefore, it is viewed with suspicion by those on the religious right, who have come to see peace as a threat to their identity.[8]

---

5. In 2000, President Clinton convened a summit at Camp David between Palestinian president Yasser Arafat and Israeli prime minister Ehud Barak.

6. Alexandria Declaration.

7. Yehezkel Landau, *Healing the Holy Land: Interreligious Peacebuilding in Israel/Palestine* (Washington, DC: U.S. Institute of Peace, 2003), 13.

8. Rabbi Melchior, interview, Jerusalem, June 1, 2010.

USIP's engagement in the process began in the wake of the Alexandria summit, when the Institute's Religion and Peacemaking Program was approached by Melchior and others involved in the process to support efforts to implement the declaration's recommendations.[9] The summit in Egypt was itself a process of interfaith dialogue, facilitated by the archbishop of Canterbury, George Carey, assisted by his special representative to the Middle East, Canon Andrew White. But what the relevant religious leaders agreed to in the declaration were broadly expressed commitments to ending the violence in the Holy Land. This all-too-rare high-level ecumenical gathering and the joint statement of principles and recommendations that these leaders forged had a deeply symbolic value, but it was just the beginning. If the ultimate goals of the initiative were to be realized, ongoing efforts were required. Accordingly, the final stipulation among the seven points articulated in the document provided for "the establishment of a permanent joint committee to carry out the recommendations of this declaration, and to engage with our respective political leadership accordingly."[10] A Permanent Committee for the Implementation of the Alexandria Declaration (PCIAD) was established that broadened participation in the process beyond the original signatories to include spiritual leaders within their respective religious communities.

This process of implementation has been a mixed bag, as discussed further. Any evaluation of its strengths and shortcomings, however, requires an understanding of how the declaration was forged. The group of Jewish, Muslim, and Christian leaders who came together in Alexandria in January 2002 included Rabbi Eliyahu Bakshi-Doron, the Sephardi chief rabbi of Israel, Michel Sabbah, the Latin patriarch in Jerusalem, and Sheikh Tal El-Sider, minister of state for the Palestinian Authority.[11] However, the meeting chaired by Carey and hosted by the grand sheikh of Al Azhar University, Sheikh Mohammed Sayed Tantawi, followed a series of preliminary meetings that had taken place with the backing of the president of the Palestinian Authority, Yasser Arafat, and the prime minister of Israel, Ariel Sharon. Once the idea of a summit had traction and buy-in

---

9. Despite offers of funding from the Palestinian and Israeli governments, the principals of Alexandria opted to take only international support (in addition to USIP, the British and U.S. governments, Coventry Cathedral, and the Norwegian Church have been primary supporters. (see Andrew White, "Bringing Religious Leaders Together in Israel/Palestine," in *Religious Contributions to Peacemaking: When Religion Brings Peace, Not War*, edited by David Smock [Washington, DC: U.S. Institute of Peace, 2006]), 9–10.

10. Alexandria Declaration.

11. Sheikh El-Sider was considered a key presence at the summit. Formerly a Hamas sympathizer, El-Sider became an ardent believer in the power of religion as a tool to bring about peace and reconciliation.

from key religious and political leaders, Melchior, El-Sider, Rabbi David Rosen,[12] Rabbi Menachem Froman,[13] and Canon White worked on an initial draft of the statement that was to become the First Alexandria Declaration of the Religious Leaders of the Holy Land. The document took shape over the course of a few weeks, crafted collectively at a series of late-night meetings at the Mount Zion hotel in Jerusalem.[14] According to White, this process was a true cooperative effort, and while those participating had not previously engaged in such a process, it was one marked by productivity, good will, and relative ease. Rosen corroborates this characterization of the preparatory meetings, attributing it in large part to the commitment and personality of El-Sider.[15] Others, such as Sheikh Taisir Tamimi, chief justice of the Palestinian sharia courts and one of the key leaders participating in the summit, also saw the draft and weighed in with suggested amendments. By the time the summit occurred, the text had been not only vetted by key representatives to the meeting but also approved by Arafat and Sharon.

The goal of drafting a mutually agreeable text was a challenge, but by the separate accounts of Melchior, Rosen, and White, this initial drafting process was characterized by good relations and remarkable buy-in from the participants. The second stipulation of the declaration proved to be one formula for engendering consensus. Crafted by Rosen, it calls on Palestinians and Israelis to "respect the divinely ordained purposes of the Creator by whose grace they live in the same land that is called Holy." According to Rosen, using religiously providential language was the key to buy-in: although consensus was harder to come by when delving into "the political nitty gritty," no one wanted to challenge language that spoke of divine providence.[16]

Rosen's point is well illustrated by what transpired at the summit where the Anglican and Roman Catholic representatives, along with Tamimi,

---

12. Rosen is the international director of interreligious affairs of the American Jewish Committee and its Heilbrunn Institute for International Interreligious Understanding. In addition to being a key driver and shaper of the Alexandria Declaration, he has long been involved in interfaith relations, serving as advisor on interreligious affairs to the Chief Rabbinate of Israel, and on the latter's Commission for Interreligious Relations.

13. Froman is a long-time advocate of Jewish-Muslim dialogue and peace activist from the West Bank Jewish settlement of Tekoa. El-Sidr has attributed his evolution from Hamas sympathizer to activist for religious peacemaking, in part, to ongoing dialogue with Froman and attributes the success of forging the Alexandria Declaration to the relationship between the two men (see Landau, *Healing the Holy Land*, 17).

14. Although all stakeholders to the declaration were invited to participate in the preparation of the document before the summit, the Palestinian Christians were not as involved in the initial meetings, a fact that White attributes to the day-to-day demands of running their churches.

15. Rabbi David Rosen, telephone interview, May 10, 2010; Canon Andrew White, telephone interview, March 8, 2012.

16. Rosen, interview, 2010.

argued forcefully for changes to the text to include language of Israeli occupation of Palestinian land. For the Jewish representatives, including such a reference would provocatively politicize a text that sought to seek common ground. According to White, deadlock around this discussion at the summit threatened to thwart the process, Carey eventually telling White that he had two more hours to get agreement before it would be necessary to announce that the summit had failed to reach its goal. Ultimately, it was Sir John Sawer, the United Kingdom's ambassador to Egypt, who came up with a formula that broke the impasse and led to the declaration's issuance.[17]

After the summit, in October 2002, Carey chaired a meeting of the committee at Lambeth Palace—the official London residence of the archbishop of Canterbury. The primary goals were for the delegates to reaffirm their commitment to the declaration, to discuss a strategy for implementation with an eye to how PCIAD's work might feed into the political process, to weigh the possibility of creating a form of crisis-response mechanism to address episodes of interfaith tension that threatened to boil over, and to decide on the timeliness of talks over the status of Jerusalem and the Holy Places. A ten-point implementation plan emerged from that meeting, but the generalities of the plan—"to systematically work through the implementation of the Alexandria Declaration; to provide encouragement for the delegates . . . to continue the bold work that they have started"[18]— suggest a lack of clear direction for the initiative that manifested itself in the follow-up process. Several factors account for this but among them appears to be a lack of clarity regarding who was to take the lead post-Alexandria—the local leaders or Archbishop Carey. According to Canon Trond Bakkevig[19]—the convener of the post-Alexandria creation, the Council of Religious Institutions of the Holy Land—in the follow-up to the Alexandria meeting, the religious leaders looked to Carey for direction.[20] However, whereas White was to remain engaged in his position as the archbishopric's special representative to the Middle East, when PCIAD met at Lambeth Palace, Carey was in the last days of his tenure as archbishop, and therefore his continued commitment was uncertain.

17. White, interview, 2012.

18. Landau, *Healing the Holy Land*, 20.

19. Bakkevig is a pastor of the Church of Norway and has served an adviser to the general secretary of the Lutheran World Federation. He has been heavily engaged in interfaith peacebuilding between Christians, Muslims, and Jews in the Middle East since the 1990s. The Church of Norway was an early supporter, along with USIP, of the Alexandria process.

20. Canon Trond Bakkevig, convener of the CRIHL, interview, Washington, DC, April 29, 2010.

That said, in 2003, PCIAD met almost monthly in Jerusalem to discuss how the Alexandria process could best improve interfaith communication. The process entailed a continuous effort to expand the network of religious leaders who would sign on to the tenets enshrined in the Alexandria Declaration. According to White, each meeting of the committee was marked by a growing respect among the participants and an acknowledgment that these leaders of different faith communities were meeting as friends, rather than enemies. One such successful effort was a gathering of approximately thirty Palestinian Islamic religious leaders that took place at Al Azhar University in Cairo in January 2004. The participants included not only leaders who had been present at Alexandria but also mid-level clerics not previously involved in peacemaking efforts, along with White, Melchior, and Froman. The presence of the two rabbis made a strong impression on the Palestinian participants, for many of whom this was a first interfaith encounter. White noted the dramatic impact for the Palestinians of hearing from rabbis who sympathized with their suffering and were willing to work with them for a "just peace."[21]

Such efforts to further the process that started in Alexandria have continued. Regular meetings of PCIAD resulted in the establishment in 2005 of the Council of Religious Institutions of the Holy Land (CRIHL), a consultative body representing the highest official religious authorities in the Holy Land. The council was formed to inject some continuity into the process and aims to prevent conflict over religious sites, and to diffuse religious tensions when they flare up. In addition, Rabbi Melchior went on to found Mosaica with Elie Wiesel in 2004. As an organization that officially defines its goal with reference to the principles enshrined in the declaration, Mosaica devotes itself to interreligious cooperation between Muslims and Jews.[22] Similarly, in 2005, the Adam Centers for Dialogue between Civilizations were established in Gaza and in the Arab town of Kfar Qassem in Israel, led by two prominent Muslim sheikhs, Imad Falluji and Abdallah Nimr Darwish. Neither Falluji nor Darwish was engaged at Alexandria, and as such their presence represents a success of the follow-up process in expanding the project's reach.

---

21. Julie Stahl, "Palestinian Leaders Want to Be a Force for Peace," CNS News Service, January 14, 2004. Cited in Peter Weinberger, "Incorporating Religion into Israeli-Palestinian Peacemaking: Recommendations for Policymakers," George Mason University, 2004, http://www.gmu.edu/depts/crdc/docs/recommendations.pdf.

22. In keeping with its support of the implementation phase of the Alexandria process, USIP has funded one of Mosaica's programs devoted to dialogue between religious Zionist rabbis and sheikhs of the Southern Islamic movement within Israel.

Evaluating the Process

The Alexandria summit was the first interfaith gathering of religious leaders in the region, and the text negotiated and signed there was also the first of its kind. As such, there is an undeniable symbolic value to the declaration forged at the summit that brought the Holy Land's top leadership of the three monotheistic faiths together and the subsequent facilitation of interaction between local religious leaders that the declaration and process engendered. However, the very personality-driven process that led to Alexandria became a challenge to the ultimate goal of implementation; accordingly, in many ways the aftermath did not do justice to the initiative. As Rosen has observed, part of the strength of the Alexandria Declaration was also its weakness: ownership was personal rather than institutional.[23] White reinforces the significance of particular personalities in moving the process forward, pointing to the natural inclination toward peace and reconciliation of both El-Sider and Melchior (among others) as a key driver of the progress made early on.[24] Once those who participated in the initial stages of the process left their official positions or—as with El-Sider—died, the lack of institutional ownership left continuity in doubt.

As noted, institutions such as Mosaica, the Adam Centers, and CRIHL were established precisely to address this concern. According to White, once he went on to focus primarily on interfaith reconciliation efforts in Iraq, the work of Mosaica and the Adam Centers was seen as the mechanism for furthering the goals of Alexandria. Yet, although Mosaica and the Adam Centers remain regularly engaged in interfaith dialogue work, Mosaica's emphasis is primarily on Jewish-Muslim engagement. In Gaza, the Adam Center is severely limited in its ability to engage Jews in dialogue, a factor driven by the political reality that renders contact between Gaza and Israel practically impossible. CRIHL convenes the Chief Rabbinate, the heads of the Christian Churches in the Holy Land, and the leadership of the Palestinian Ministry of Religious Affairs and of the Sharia courts. Although CRIHL launched a project in 2009, funded by the United States Department of State, to study Israeli and Palestinian textbooks for their portrayal of the other,[25] the council has proven to be primarily a statement-issuing body, and even then member institutions are frequently reluctant to get involved

---

23. Rosen, interview, 2010.

24. White, interview, 2012.

25. See "Israeli-Palestinian Schoolbook Project," Council of Religious Institutions of the Holy Land, http://www.crihl.org/content/israeli-palestinian-schoolbook-project.

in issues too closely associated with the policy of one government or another. This is largely a function of the religious leadership on both the Jewish and Muslim sides being so closely tied to the government and, therefore, not wanting to push boundaries without the security of a mandate from the political echelons.

The religiously sanctioned cease-fire called for in the declaration and the implementation of the Mitchell and Tenet recommendations (or political agreements that superseded) remain elusive, but one cannot ignore the reverberating power of the relationship building that occurred between many of the participants in Alexandria. Although the summit focused almost exclusively on the document that was its outcome, the follow-up meetings dealt with the emergent challenges to the interfaith cooperation called for in the declaration.[26] One powerful example is White's participation in the negotiations to successfully resolve the thirty-eight-day siege of the Church of the Nativity in Bethlehem in May 2002.[27] Both White and Melchior attribute the success of this endeavor, and other post-Alexandria interventions to calm interfaith tensions, to the network of relationships forged during the Alexandria summit. The declaration has also had influence beyond the Middle East context, and been the inspiration for religious peacemaking efforts in Nigeria and postwar Iraq.

Juxtaposed as this description is with the description of the Ecumenical Women's Dialogue in Colombia described in the next section, one cannot ignore the stark contrast between these two processes in terms of approach and participation. To date, the Alexandria process has not engaged women in any of its meetings. This is a function of the nature and design of the initiative: driven by the religious leadership of the Holy Land, and facilitated by the upper echelons of the Anglican Church, this is currently doctrinally all male. The follow-up to Alexandria has focused on expanding the reach of engagement and buy-in to the process, but this has still centered primarily on clergy rather than on lay constituencies, and so the entire endeavor remains the province of men. The Colombia project offers an alternative model to interfaith dialogue—not only from a gender perspective but also in its composition of lay religious participants whose focus was not on supporting a parallel political process but rather on building trust based on shared experience and a drive to create grassroots peacebuilding initiatives on the very local level.

---

26. White, interview, 2012.

27. The siege occurred when Muslim militants holed themselves up inside the church in a standoff with the Israeli military outside.

Ecumenical Women's Dialogue in Colombia

Colombia has suffered decades of violent conflict rooted in economic and political disparity and exacerbated by drug trafficking.[28] As with the Israeli-Palestinian conflict, pinpointing an exact start is an exercise fraught with political sensitivities. Armed guerilla groups, the largest and most well-known being the Marxist-oriented Revolutionary Armed Forces of Colombia (more commonly known as the FARC), arose in the 1960s with the stated objective to achieve justice for poor rural-based Colombians who had been marginalized from political decision-making in Bogotá. The FARC has operated in and controlled areas throughout Colombia where the government has limited reach. As war dragged on over many years, a significant number of right-wing paramilitary fighters emerged, many of them landowners, claiming to take up arms to protect their local communities and put an end to the usurpation of lands by guerrilla groups. The conflict in Colombia has been marked by kidnappings, disappearances, and human rights violations; paramilitary, guerrilla-armed fighters, and the Colombian Army have all been accused of violating humanitarian law. Several attempts at negotiations between the government and armed groups have been made. Those with the guerrilla groups have failed. Following a peace deal with the largest paramilitary group, the United Self Defense Forces of Colombia (the AUC), more than 30,000 paramilitary have participated in a demobilization process since 2003.

In recent years, developments in Colombia's conflict situation have been noteworthy, particularly several strategic gains by the government against the FARC. This includes the 2008 capture of key political hostages held by the FARC, including former presidential candidate Ingrid Betancourt. However, peace negotiations with the FARC and the second-largest rebel group, the National Liberation Army (ELN), have stalled. Meanwhile, violence continues to escalate in some parts of the country as demobilized paramilitary disturb local communities.

The Colombian population is roughly 90 percent Catholic, and the Catholic Church has been heavily involved in efforts to bring peace to the beleaguered country.[29] Catholic bishops and priests have served as principal intermediaries between armed actors at both the local and the national level, and leadership within the Catholic Church pursues comprehensive peace

---

28. This project was similarly reviewed in Hayward, "Peace through Inter and Intra Religious Dialogue."

29. Hector Fabio Henao Gaviria, "The Colombian Church and Peacebuilding," in *Colombia: Building Peace in a Time of War*, edited by Virginia Bouvier (Washington, DC: U.S. Institute of Peace, 2009).

and justice programming.[30] Catholic women and the minority Protestant communities, both mainline and Pentecostal denominations, have also been operating in some of the most conflict-affected parts of the country to build peace and bring humanitarian assistance and empowerment to the displaced and other victims of conflict. These religiously motivated peacemakers, working through local churches, their religious orders, or faith-based organizations, often have an intimate understanding of local conflict dynamics and have been able to create effective community-based programs to build pockets of peace and justice. Despite their impressive work, Catholic and Protestant peacemakers face historical tensions between their communities that can hamper effective partnership.

The conflict divide in Colombia is not across Catholic and Protestant lines, nor is religion a compelling driver of the conflict. Nonetheless, in this complex Colombian conflict, tensions and divisions between these two communities have grown (as they have among many civil society groups). This has created challenges for grassroots peacebuilders seeking to create broad coalitions to tackle the complex and deeply rooted problems their society is facing. In response to this situation, USIP has supported the creation of a network of Catholic and Protestant women peacebuilders throughout Colombia. This example highlights the importance of intrafaith dialogue—or dialogue among groups within a particular religious tradition. Some argue that intrafaith dialogue can be even more challenging to facilitate than interfaith dialogue. After all, when engaging across religious traditions, one is prepared to encounter significant points of disagreement or difference. But when communities within the same tradition have competing interpretations of that tradition, and when the shared set of basic religious beliefs leads denominational communities to competing political, economic, or social objectives, real anxiety and tension are both possible and likely, and require particularly sensitive facilitation.

The Process

In 2006, USIP developed relationships with Catholic and Protestant leaders involved in peace efforts in Colombia, and learned about tensions between the groups that had frustrated collective work in the past. Several leaders suggested that USIP might serve as an appropriate neutral convener

---

30. CIA World Factbook, "Colombia," https://www.cia.gov/library/publications/the-world-factbook/geos/co.html.

of the two communities. After further visits and discussions, USIP found that women involved in peace efforts through their religious communities were leading particularly exciting initiatives and were especially eager to engage more deeply in ecumenical work, much of which in the past had been led by men. As such, since 2008, USIP has supported a dialogue process between Catholic and Protestant women who are involved in peacebuilding throughout Colombia. The dual purposes of the initiative are to build ecumenical relationships with a goal of creating a broader movement of faith-based peacebuilders in Colombia, and to affirm and strengthen the role of women in peacebuilding.

Two organizations were approached to lead this initiative—one from each community. On the Protestant side is Justapaz, a Mennonite peacebuilding organization that works closely with the wider Protestant community, both mainline and Pentecostal, and is significantly involved in the major national organizing body of Protestants (CEDECOL). On the Catholic side, the Conferencia Episcopal de Colombia (CEC), the national office of Catholic bishops, lent its support, and the woman invited to lead the effort represented the Conferencia de Religiosos y Religiosas de Colombia, a body that organizes the many Catholic religious orders throughout the country. A steering committee with equal number of Protestant and Catholic representatives was created and the first step of the initiative conceived: to hold a national gathering of Catholic and Protestant women peacebuilders from throughout Colombia over several days to build relationships and share best practices. Over the coming months, the steering committee met regularly to design and prepare for the symposium. For the most part, USIP offered support from afar—encouraging the process, asking questions, and ensuring an equal sharing of decision-making and responsibilities between the two communities.

The first symposium was held in November 2008. The mood was festive, hopeful, and energetic. The emphasis was on setting the right tone and encouraging commitment to the continued process. As such, participants did not discuss sensitive issues dividing the communities. Instead, the group discussed common problems women face in Colombian society and presented their successful peacebuilding initiatives. Large group presentations, small group discussions, and brainstorming were broken up by meaningful moments of shared worship, dance, prayer, and play. By the conclusion, the women had affirmed the need to build relationships between Catholics and Protestants, the worth of working ecumenically to build peace, and the particular role that women can play in advancing these goals. They made a commitment to advance the national movement and to ground it in the varying regional experiences of conflict.

Following the inaugural symposium, however, little progress was made. Although the first gathering had—rightly—not delved into specifics or engaged difficult and sensitive topics out of a desire to first establish relationships and an environment of trust, the lack of specific commitments resulted in lack of clarity about next steps. The steering committee members became preoccupied with their concurrent peace and justice projects managed through their own organizations. As a result, the project languished.

After several months of inaction, tensions arose between the coordinators and within the network. USIP was approached separately by both communities, each expressing frustration—either because of the lack of forward progress or because they felt others were being unduly impatient. Recognizing that the original good will and constructive engagement had hit a hurdle, USIP decided to travel to Colombia and spend several days with both the steering committee and members of the wider network to facilitate dialogue between the two groups.

During a four-day workshop outside Bogotá, USIP first invited them to reflect on and celebrate the strides they had already taken together, which restored a sense of optimism. It then facilitated discussion within and between the communities about what peace means to them, what are their priorities in building this vision of peace, and how these beliefs stem from their religious convictions. This provided the members greater clarity about the common ground and differences in approach between them, and introduced them to religious understandings specific to their different traditions. USIP then carefully led them in discussion of the tensions preventing them from advancing their work together. USIP met with each community separately, allowing them to speak openly and honestly about their frustrations and fears, and then brought them together and helped them share these concerns with each other. Some of these fears related to backlash they might face (or had already faced) from their communities for their ecumenical peace work, but other fears were related to dynamics internal to the network. In particular, many expressed concern that they had been, or would be, disrespected or looked down on by women in the other community, not shown appreciation for differences in religious belief or commitment. After surfacing these fears and ensuring that the two communities heard and acknowledged them, USIP helped the participants devise a set of guidelines for their continued work together. These guidelines sought to address their fears and ensure processes and commitments to maintain open communication and respectful engagement. Finally, USIP trained them to facilitate similar ecumenical dialogues within their local communities, describing for them the techniques we had used in the workshop, presenting several other models, and giving them opportunities to practice facilitating small group discussions.

In the end, this intervention successfully reinvigorated the project. Key to its success was both the timing, a moment when both sides recognized the need to reengage with vigor and address tensions or risk the demise of the project, and the process of this intervention, a combination of dialogue and training. This process met two concurrent needs: for the groups to voice their fears and needs related to the project—which simultaneously addressed intrafaith bias and promoted greater understanding of the different traditions—and for participants to feel they were gaining skills in the initiative that would be useful to them in their own peace work. This assured them that their continued efforts with the initiative would benefit them in concrete ways.

Following this intervention, leaders in the network conducted regional consultations throughout Colombia. In each region, the leaders worked with local network members to hold a series of meetings and dialogical encounters between Catholic and Protestant communities. These meetings surfaced local conflict-related issues facing women and provided space for participants (primarily but not exclusively women) to discuss drivers of tension and bias between Protestant and Catholic communities. The regional consultations gave network members opportunities to try their own hand at facilitating ecumenical dialogue, putting into practice what they had learned in the workshop. It also allowed the network's Bogotá-based leaders to better understand the needs, concerns, and successes of women outside Bogotá. Currently the leadership is aiming for a second national gathering at which the wider network will seek to clearly define and embrace its mission, administration and decision-making process, and short- and long-term goals moving forward—goals that take into account both regional and national needs.

Evaluating the Process

The Ecumenical Women Peacebuilders project in Colombia, though not without challenges, was a relatively successful model for a multiyear grassroots intrafaith dialogical encounter. It made clear progress toward its goals of empowering women peacebuilders and bridging their relationship across the Protestant-Catholic divide. The women involved have frequently cited the deepening of their relationship with, and understanding of, one another, their affirmation as important builders of peace in Colombia, the acquisition of skills and ideas to support their peace work, and multiple ecumenical peacebuilding activities that have stemmed from this initiative.

USIP's sensitivity to, and management of, several dynamics within the network was key. First, USIP anticipated that power imbalances between the communities in the wider society would manifest in the dialogical encounter. In Colombia, Catholics hold greater power and influence than the often poorer and marginalized Protestant communities. They also have greater access to resources for their work. This power imbalance caused tension and defensiveness among the participants and sometimes challenged the project's momentum, particularly when Protestant members felt they were being pushed by the Catholics into particular activities. USIP remained conscious of these power imbalances from the beginning, always engaging the two communities on an evenhanded basis and taking care to ensure parity of responsibility and decision-making. For example, rather than send all project funds to either Justapaz or the Conferencia de Religiosos y Religiosas de Colombia, USIP split the funds evenly between them and worked with both organizations to designate a clear process for project implementation that ensured shared responsibility. In implementing the project in this intentionally evenhanded way, USIP sought to balance the power differential. In individual and small group encounters, USIP also pointed out these power dynamics to the leadership so that they would become sensitive to them in their collective work moving forward.

Throughout the implementation, it was critical for USIP to manage the two communities' expectations regarding pacing, joint action, and topics for discussion. As alluded to earlier, the Catholics were often eager for the group to engage in joint collective action. Before joining the network, many of the Catholic members had been involved for years in the peacebuilding, human rights, and social outreach work of the Church, and had a theology undergirding this work. By contrast, many of the Protestant community members, particularly those from the Pentecostal community, were newer to the work of peace and justice. They often requested more time to deliberate the theological and scriptural foundation of these issues, and they wrestled with how the community should be engaged in social and political issues, if at all. The Pentecostal members were generally less enthusiastic about advocacy work, preferring instead to focus on social-psychological support to their community through pastoral outreach and Bible study with victims and former combatants.[31] These competing differences caused real tensions between the members, even leading some to drop out of the initiative. As facilitator, USIP had to balance these competing needs, highlight them for the group, and help them consider how to respond to both communities' needs in moving forward.

Similarly, USIP sought to ensure that the Catholics' developed theology and practical program of peacebuilding did not become the de facto theology and action of the group. Because the Catholic members generally had more experience with peace work, the mentality in the dialogue was sometimes to grant them the authority to define the issues and necessary response. This mentality has disempowered the Protestant community, however, by silencing its experience and unique, if nascent, theology of peacebuilding. The Pentecostal traditions may not have been historically as involved in traditional peacebuilding work—particularly human rights or advocacy work—but they have been engaged in social outreach and pastoral work they believe contributes to sustainable peace. Part of the USIP role as facilitator was to ensure that neither group's definition of peace and peacebuilding trumped, and that all equally contributed to the emergence of an authentically ecumenical conceptual basis for their joint work.

At the same time, however, the lack of a specific definition of peace and peacebuilding was a weakness. The Alexandria process, responding as it did to the Oslo Accords, had a more specific set of objectives and a narrow understanding of peacemaking associated with the formal negotiations. The divergent understandings of peace and peacebuilding between the two communities, and even among individual members on the steering committee and in the wider network, made it difficult for the group to focus on specific issues and devise concrete action plans. In this way, the attempt to conceive an inclusive and broad definition of peace created a challenge when it came to discerning specific objectives and activities the group could pursue together.

One of the biggest challenges in facilitating this project was that much was done from afar. USIP does not have an office in Colombia and was thus unable to provide regular face-to-face engagement or to respond directly, in person, when a hurdle arose in the process. Shuttle diplomacy between the groups to understand and mediate disagreements was often conducted by email or telephone. This, at times, created real difficulties and led to prolong-

---

31. There were times when Pentecostal members highlighted activities they considered peacebuilding but which do not fit appropriate definitions—in particular, activities whose primary purpose was evangelism or proselytism. The dialogue space became a safe arena for the women to discuss how these activities contribute to peace or to inter-communal tensions. They included in their guidelines for their collective work a prohibition against proselytism.

ing tensions or problems that might otherwise have been ameliorated earlier, and thus the attrition of some participants impatient about lack of progress in the face of unresolved issues. Ideally, facilitators of a process like this must engage early and often, both in group and in one-on-one meetings, with both the leaders and participants from the group to pick up on and address dynamics that could stymie the group's progress.

Lessons Learned

In evaluating these two studies, several lessons emerge that may be more generally instructive for IFD. Among the important lessons already noted are the need for sustained dialogues and long-term commitment from participants or organizations, clarity on the process of implementation and objectives, and the need to tailor IFD process and topics to meet the leverage and interest of participants.

Additionally, the Colombian example underscores the power of nonverbal communication. In these ecumenical encounters, prayer, shared worship, and ritual played an essential role. All dialogue sessions began with worship and prayer, and particularly at moments of catharsis or heightened tension, the group paused for prayer or song. Biblical stories—particularly those relating to women in the Bible who were victims of violence or served as leaders in their communities—were read and dramatized. Art and dance were integrated into the encounters. Responsibility for designing and leading these aspects of the encounter was always jointly shared. In some instances, Catholic and Protestant women worked together to design and lead the worship, at other times they took turns, but in every instance they worshiped collectively. These moments were essential to building relationships. In fact, the participants often pointed to shared worship as the most transformative or inspiring aspect of their encounter. These moments keep the women from being dragged down psychologically or spiritually by the weighty discursive work of dialogue.

The Colombian example is also instructive with regard to the dynamics of facilitating dialogues between majority and minority communities. Participants from the majority Catholic community often preferred to dialogue about similarities between the communities; they became anxious when the group focused on differences, fearing that doing so would divide the group. Meanwhile, the minority Protestant community often preferred to spend more time asserting and exploring differences within the group, seeking to explain their unique contributions that differed from the norm in society, a norm often defined by the majority community. In other words, when the dialogue only focused on commonalities, the minorities felt that their unique contributions were being ignored or dismissed, and they become anxious or resentful.

By contrast to the Colombia project, the Alexandria process highlights one of the challenges of a dialogue process driven by high-profile political leaders. Such individuals frequently feel constrained by their position and unable to freely engage in the type of deep exploration and self-analysis that is optimally required for a facilitated dialogue process to reap benefits. Leaders also have constituencies to which they are answerable. It is therefore tempting for them to engage in political positioning and one-upmanship, making trust building a challenge for the facilitator. As described earlier, at the summit in 2002, despite prior consultation and vetting of the text by most of the participants, heated negotiations over the language almost resulted in a failed endeavor. It is worth considering the role played here by the pressures that some of the leaders felt once in the room and charged with producing a public document to which their names would be attached. On the flip side, these two case studies analyzed side by side highlight the distinct challenges associated with engaging elites or engaging grassroots communities. Although the highly visible and political roles of some of the participants in Alexandria constrained their work, precisely because the process involved such high-level leaders, the symbolic impact, visibility, and reach were significant. By contrast, the Colombian women, despite the possibility of backlash they might face from their religious communities, nonetheless had a great deal more flexibility in engagement and could speak openly without fear of crossing any "institutional line." However, the symbolic impact of their encounter was hardly felt by the larger Colombian civil society, and their work was limited to very local efforts.

Likewise, Alexandria exemplifies the limitations of a dialogue initiative so intimately tied to a political process and dependent on political movement for success. Rosen has expressed his own view that the capacity for community buy-in to Alexandria will depend on progress being made on the political front. In an interview with Yehezkel Landau, he described the constraints of the religious leaders who are political appointees in the Holy Land. "They are not independent actors. . . . In meetings like the one in Alexandria, each side appeals to the other to get the adversary's political leaders behind a credible peace plan. And the other side responds, 'If you would get your political leaders to change, then we would have a better chance of influencing our own.' "[32] At the same time, Alexandria points to the power of personal relationship

---

32. Cited in Landau, *Healing the Holy Land*, 24.

building to overcome some of those challenges. Palestinian participants in the PCIAD follow-on sessions were frequently held up or prevented from coming to the meetings because Israel withheld the needed permissions for travel. When those who had been delayed at checkpoints finally arrived, the grim realities of the political situation to which they had been subjected would taint their mood and dampen the fervor for cooperation. However, as White attests, what would frequently turn this situation around was when these same Palestinians saw how hard the Israeli participants worked to convince their own authorities to let the Palestinians get to the meetings. On one occasion, when Tamimi was prevented from traveling, Melchior traveled with White to the West Bank to personally apologize to him.[33]

Finally, as with the Colombian example, unequal power dynamics among the participants can be a complicating factor. The Christian representatives engaged in Alexandria are a far more diverse group of actors than their Jewish and Muslim counterparts, representing several denominations whose interests are not perfectly aligned.[34] According to both Bakkevig and White, they also suffer from being perceived as playing a secondary or more intermediary role between the Jews and Muslims as opposed to being an equal stakeholder. As noted in regard to the valuable work being pursued by Mosaica, frequently the trilateral aspect of Alexandria has been lost in the follow-up, subsumed by Jewish-Muslim dynamics.

Conclusion

Facilitated religious dialogue is not a panacea for conflict generally, or for religious conflict more specifically. Conflict often arises from and is sustained by structural injustices or poor governance, which cannot be transformed by dialogue alone. Interfaith dialogue, like all facilitated dialogue, works best when integrated into comprehensive peacebuilding projects that address the "hard" as well as "soft" aspects of peacebuilding.

When integrated into or coordinated with other peacebuilding work, IFD can be extremely useful in creating a foundation for joint action to reduce violence. It can strengthen such initiatives by deepening the relationships between those involved and ensuring open and regular communication between them. IFD can also be useful for conflict prevention by strengthening relationships between communities and thereby decreasing the potential for communal divides to become fault lines of violence. When conflict breaks

---

33. White, interview, 2012.
34. Bakkevig, interview, 2010.

out between the communities, those who have been involved in IFD can reach across to their contacts from the other tradition to resolve the conflict before it breaks into violence. Finally, IFD can be used to strengthen cultural and institutional commitments to religious, ethnic, racial, and communal pluralism. Although greater evaluation is needed to understand when IFD is appropriate, and how it can be most effective, IFD's contribution to building global peace and security has been testified to in numerous UN resolutions and the work of USIP over several decades.[35]

---

35. United Nations General Assembly Resolutions 58/128, 59/23, 60/10, and 61/221 all call for inter-religious dialogue and cooperation as a necessary means to promote a global culture of peace. Other United Nations forums and bodies, including the Tripartite Forum on Interfaith Cooperation for Peace and the Alliance for Civilizations, confirm the worth of interfaith dialogue as a tool for strength-ening international human rights and peace (for more on interfaith dialogue work, including further description of USIP's work, see Smock, *Interfaith Dialogue and Peacemaking*; Smock, *Religious Contri-butions to Peacemaking*; Landau, *Healing the Holy Land*).

5

Colombia: Civil Society Dialogues for Peace

Virginia M. Bouvier

A s part of its work to promote conflict transformation, in Colombia as elsewhere, USIP has been facilitating a series of dialogues to create spaces for civil society leaders to discuss, define, and articulate strategies for peace in the country; to build relationships and networks to put peace on the agenda of U.S. nongovernmental organizations (NGOs) and policymakers; and to ensure that U.S. policies better support Colombian efforts to secure peace. The evolution of this process has included three phases, marked by major meetings in December 2008, December 2009, and August 2010, with smaller meetings throughout this period. This chapter evaluates each phase, reviews the challenges that emerged and how they were addressed, and offers some preliminary lessons from the Colombian case on managing and carrying out facilitated dialogues in conflict zones.

For the purposes of this chapter, facilitated dialogue refers to an intentional process to shape a dialogue among parties. The facilitator is the process leader. His or her role consists of both preparing the parties for engagement and then facilitating the dialogue, which can be a series of conversations. The facilitator's role in the pre-dialogue stage includes consulting with the parties and other stakeholders to identify who should be engaged in the dialogues, setting the parameters of the substance to be discussed, convening the dialogues, eliciting inputs from participants on the nature of the problem to be addressed, assessing areas of agreement and disagreement, helping move the discussion toward action plans, and helping design follow-up mechanisms. The dialogues are safe spaces where new ideas can be tested, and relationships among participants built or strengthened. They are a place for stepping back from the day-to-day press of events to evaluate the nature of the problem and the challenges faced, and to design collective solutions.

Facilitation, unlike mediation, generally implies less responsibility for producing outcomes and more focus on the process itself as a model for conflict resolution. The facilitator is also responsible for ensuring oversight for the implementation and verification of agreements reached during the process.

Background

Colombia's internal armed conflict has lasted for more than six decades. The 1948 killing of Jorge Eliecer Gaitán, a popular Liberal reformer, sparked intense partisan violence between the Liberal and Conservative parties and resulted in the deaths of more than 200,000 people. The violence was temporarily staunched when a power-sharing agreement that alternated power between the two parties was reached. Today's internal armed conflict is rooted in the violence of this early period, when the consolidation of power in the hands of a small exclusive ruling elite firmed up practices of political, social, and economic exclusion that give Colombia one of the highest rates of inequality in the world today.

In Colombia, the standard mechanisms and procedures of democracy—elections, ballots, voting, institutions to provide protection and accountability—exist side by side with a state characterized by a consistently poor human rights record, violence and intimidation, corruption, clientelism, exclusion, and discrimination. Efforts to create progressive third-party alternatives, including the recently formed Polo Democrático Alternativo, have been met with repression, harassment, legal and bureaucratic obstacles, and defamation.[1]

Poverty, injustice, inequities, and a lack of legitimate avenues for change gave rise to the emergence of some thirteen guerrilla groups, beginning in the 1960s. Many of these demobilized at the end of the twentieth century, but two remain active. The larger, the Revolutionary Armed Forces of Colombia (FARC), was founded by Manuel Marulanda to represent the demands of a rural peasantry. The smaller National Liberation Army (ELN) represented the demands for change of educated, urban youths inspired by the Cuban Revolution and the tenets of liberation theology.

---

1. The PDA is currently battling a legal maneuver to prohibit it from presenting candidates or voting in the 2011 congressional elections due to its abstention in the 2010 presidential runoff elections. Presidential candidates of the left—including Luis Carlos Galán, Carlos Pizarro, and Bernardo Jaramillo (the latter two representing guerrilla groups that sought a political role following their demobilization) have been killed, as were some three thousand members of the Union Patriótica, the political party led by Jaramillo.

In tandem with these two guerrilla groups, so-called self-defense forces also emerged, aligned in the rural areas with large landowners. By 1997, these regional paramilitary networks had converged to form a national umbrella organization they called the United Self-Defense Forces of Colombia (AUC). Collusion of paramilitary forces with regional political and economic elites and public security forces resulted in a dirty war marked by massacres, disappearances, assassinations, torture, intimidation, and displacement of community leaders who threatened the status quo.[2]

Since the 1990s, the illegal drug trade has played an ever-increasing role in the violence. The narcotics industry is underwriting the war economy, funding the armed actors and undermining their ideological origins, enabling the conflict to spread and escalate, and serving as an obstacle to the conflict's resolution.

During a particularly severe economic crisis in the mid-1990s, the violence in Colombia intensified and civil society mounted a campaign for peace that garnered 10 million votes for peace and brought Andrés Pastrana to power on a promise to seek an end to the war. In 1998, President Pastrana initiated a dialogue with the FARC. When peace talks with the FARC broke down four years later, however, civil society groups working for peace found themselves without a roadmap for moving ahead.[3] A disillusioned public embraced the presidency of Alvaro Uribe, who pledged all-out war against the guerrillas.

Initiating the Dialogues

In 2008, when this project began, the Colombian government denied the existence of an internal armed conflict, preferring to characterize the violence as terrorism. Violence had forced more than 380,000 individuals to abandon their homes, bringing the number of internally displaced to 4.6 million for the period from 1985 to 2008—second only to Sudan. The FARC and ELN had both been hard hit by the heightened military action under President Uribe's so-called democratic security policy, but the policy instrument left little room for legitimate dissent. Following the demobilization of some 30,000 paramilitary combatants of the AUC in the first decade of the

2. Latin American Working Group Education Fund, *Breaking the Silence: In Search of Colombia's Disappeared*, December 2010, http://www.lawg.org/action-center/lawg-blog/69-general/810-breaking-the-silence-in-search-of-colombias-disappeared.

3. Adam Isacson and Jorge Rojas Rodriguez, "Origins, Evolution, and Lessons of the Colombian Peace Movement," in *Colombia: Building Peace in a Time of War*, edited by Virginia M. Bouvier (Washington, DC: U.S. Institute of Peace, 2009), 19–37.

twenty-first century, new decentralized criminal gangs proliferated, complicating prospects for peace by linking together thousands of demobilized and active paramilitaries and narco-traffickers who engaged in practices of social cleansing and intimidation of social leaders and autonomous organizations. Furthermore, dozens of elected officials, including about a third of the Colombian congress, had been indicted and at least a dozen convicted for collaborating with mafias and paramilitary groups. The state's primary intelligence agency, DAS, was under attack for illegal wiretapping, intimidation, smear campaigns, and surveillance of human rights groups, journalists, Supreme Court justices and magistrates, opposition politicians, and labor leaders—some of whom were simultaneously under government protection. Those who spoke out against the violence, denounced state actions, called for peace, or tried to mediate between armed groups were subjected to intimidation, attack, or criminalization by the state.[4]

In this context, Jorge Rojas, the director of the Consultancy on Human Rights and Displacement (CODHES), a leading human rights organization in Colombia, approached USIP to see whether it might facilitate a dialogue among peace and human rights leaders in Colombia. He underscored the vulnerability of human rights workers, the relentless pace of the work, and the deep social divisions from a conflict that had lasted more than half a century—all of which were impeding civil society's ability to come together to develop a consensus on a vision or strategy for peace.

The dialogue to be facilitated was not conceptualized as one between armed actors. Rather, it was meant to provide a space for civil society leaders to reflect on their efforts to build peace, to share ideas and reflections about their work, and to strategize jointly about how their work might be more effective. Conditions seemed appropriate for third-party engagement, given the window of opportunity that was opening with the entry of new government in the White House. An invitation for USIP to serve as a facilitator was a logical first step. Such a letter would provide a mandate that legitimized USIP's role, help give direction to the process, and ensure that participants would welcome, or at least be open to, third-party engagement. The director of CODHES estimated that some forty groups would be interested in participating and agreed to draft a letter and circulate it for the appropriate signatures.

4. Lawsuits have been filed against Gloria Inés Ramírez, Wilson Borja, Álvaro Leyva, Carlos Lozano, Piedad Córdoba, the journalists Hollman Morris and William Para, as well as foreigners who have pursued contact with armed groups for humanitarian ends.

Such dialogues have been tried intermittently in Colombia under a variety of names. Generally, however, these dialogues formed temporary coalitions that lost momentum after the initial enthusiasm of coming together. They broke down into disagreements, lost their focus, were superseded by other agendas, became politicized, fizzled into inertia, disappeared as the peace processes that they were designed to support folded, or collapsed in the absence of sustainable funding.

Despite repeated promises over several months, the end of the fiscal year approached and no invitation had appeared. The earmarked funds, about $30,000, for "civil society dialogues" were under threat of being diverted to another project. When the Colombia Committee for Human Rights (CCHR) inquired about funding for a small conference in Washington, D.C., to bring together academics and policymakers to discuss U.S. policy toward Colombia, it was suggested that they consider partnering with CODHES and using the meeting as a way to bring Colombian civil society leaders together at USIP. Within a few days, CCHR presented a proposal on behalf of the two organizations for a one-day conference to take place at USIP the month after the U.S. presidential elections of 2008.

The CCHR had incorporated as a 501(c)3 organization in 1986 and had worked with many U.S. NGOs to focus attention on the human rights and humanitarian issues in Colombia. Their network of volunteers had provided hospitality, translation, accompaniment, and solidarity to the Colombian human rights community for decades. CODHES was based in Bogotá, with reach throughout Colombia and an advocacy orientation at the national level on issues of human rights and displacement. Its leader is a respected, charismatic individual with political savvy, deep connections (particularly within progressive sectors), strong organizational capacity, and a global vision.

From the beginning, several agendas of the three organizations ran in parallel. CCDR's primary interest was in executing a U.S. policy–focused conference with a strong human rights component. CODHES was interested in bringing a group of civil society leaders to USIP to strategize among themselves and to present their ideas to U.S. policymakers. USIP was interested in strengthening the capacity of civil society groups to design and articulate strategies for peace that could contribute to conflict resolution in Colombia and be a resource for the new administration as it reviewed its Colombia policy.

These agendas were complementary. The United States has long been a key actor on issues of war and peace in Colombia, having heavily funded the Colombian government's war effort through Plan Colombia from 2000 on. Talking about peace and human rights in Colombia was difficult under a polarized climate that equated calls for dialogue with sympathy with the guerrillas. Combining these agendas had clear benefits. Because sectors of the NGO community in Washington are highly organized and fairly sophisticated in their understanding of U.S. policymaking, and those in Colombia are knowledgeable about and engaged in Colombian peace initiatives and peace advocacy, strengthening the ties between these NGOs could strengthen capacity within both groups and could open new opportunities for developing joint peace strategies and implementation mechanisms, as well as creating new alliances and coalitions on peace issues. The focus on U.S. policy would help the group coalesce around concrete recommendations and strategies. Finally, although similar conferences had been held on U.S. policy and human rights in Colombia, this was the first time that a large group of Colombian civil society leaders had been brought together with the express purpose of developing recommendations for U.S. peace policies.

Phase One: Washington Group Formed

The first meeting of Colombian and U.S. civil society leaders, "Promoting Peace in Colombia: Ideas for the New Administration," held at USIP offices in Washington on December 2, 2008, brought together approximately seventy roundtable participants, more than twenty of whom represented Colombian civil society. Because this first meeting was envisioned more as a conference than a facilitated dialogue, the facilitator roles were shared among the various sponsoring organizations. The selection of the participants was made by the three sponsoring organizations. CODHES proposed the initial list of Colombian invitees. CCHR, which was administering the USIP contract for the conference, monitored budgetary implications and sought to keep the number of invitees manageable. USIP and CCHR met with and solicited input from knowledgeable Colombian specialists in Washington (who would also participate in the conference), and worked with CODHES to ensure that the invitees included participants representing diverse gender, ethnic, regional, sectoral, and religious interests.

There was some ambivalence about including Colombian and U.S. government officials. The event was seen as a closed meeting among NGOs, but the desire for interlocution with the new U.S. administration was unanimous. On the other hand, relations between the Colombian government and the NGO community were strained. The Colombians wanted a safe, protected space for strategizing, but they did not want to alienate Colombian government officials further. After much discussion, representatives of both governments were invited as lunchtime speakers. The Colombian embassy declined.

The USIP conference venue could accommodate a maximum of seventy participants, and in the end, the proposed conference of thirty-five grew to the limits of the venue. Narrowing down the participant list while ensuring broad representation of key sectors proved a challenge. Once the U.S. presidential elections were held and it was clear that a new Democratic administration would be coming into office, the demand for seats at the table grew in proportion to a widespread expectation that a new administration would be receptive to the ideas that the conference might generate. The budget and space limitations forced us to turn away potential participants. The final group from Colombia included about thirty representatives of peace, human rights, social, academic, business, political, labor, ethnic, and religious organizations. It was primarily a Bogotá-based group but included organizations with roots and branches in different regions of Colombia.

The invitees on the U.S. side were chosen in consultation with a small group of Washington-based Colombia experts and colleagues in both the executive branch and church and faith-based organizations. Criteria for selection were largely related to bureaucratic function; personal interest, experience, or expertise; and involvement in designing current programs or activities related to Colombia. A number of USIP senior fellows and staff with expertise in peacebuilding were also included. The final list of attendees from the United States included seven representatives of the U.S. government; academics from eight universities; and representatives of more than a dozen U.S. NGOs, think tanks, donors, and international organizations.

Once the Colombian participants had been selected, they were invited to submit short statements of what they saw as the key challenges for peace in Colombia and their recommendations for U.S. policymakers. Ten invitees (many of whom could not attend) submitted statements. The texts were reproduced and circulated during the conference.

The conference program was dictated by the particular political context in which it occurred—namely, the imminent inauguration of a new administration in Washington. USIP and CODHES co-moderated the program and, following introductory remarks, participants introduced themselves.

In the morning, Colombian and U.S. analysts opened the discussion on the status of different actors in the conflict and the challenges and opportunities for Colombian peacemaking. Over lunch, a high-level official from the U.S. State Department gave a short keynote address followed by discussion of the particular challenges of U.S. policies in Colombia. The afternoon focused on the role of the United States and relevant opportunities for the incoming administration to support peace in Colombia. Opening speakers included a Republican staffer from the Senate Foreign Relations Committee and a Democratic staffer from the House side, a well-respected Latin Americanist in line for one of the State Department's Latin America posts, and a longtime Colombia analyst from a U.S. nonprofit.

Participants discussed the declining U.S. influence with respect to other international actors. Many believed that the United States, particularly since Plan Colombia, had contributed to the militarization of the conflict, but there was a general sense that the United States is a key player in the path toward peace. "Peace passes through the United States," one participant remarked. Others noted that the U.S. embassy had played a key role in securing the dismissal of twenty-seven army officials involved in the scandalous "false positives" incident, when army officials had killed poor peasant youths and dressed them up as guerrillas to elevate body counts. Most agreed that the U.S. position on peace in Colombia was pivotal, and argued that Colombia offered the incoming Obama administration an opportunity to take a clear and unequivocal stance on the side of human rights and democracy in Latin America with relatively little political cost.

The group concurred that the violence and the displacements it had generated, as well as human rights violations and particularly attacks on human rights workers, had been intensifying. They hoped that the new Obama administration would be responsive to these concerns, and would elevate human rights and peace in its policy priorities. Members of the group urged the U.S. government to recognize that a state of internal armed conflict (a status the Colombian government denied) existed in Colombia, and to pursue a negotiated settlement with the FARC and ELN guerrillas. How this would be done and who the key interlocutors might be was the subject of some discussion, and many concrete ideas were suggested.

The group recognized that to design policies that promote peace, direction from civil society in Colombia needed to be more clear about what was wanted and how to achieve it. Several ideas, such as a call for a special envoy, were floated, but did not get much traction. U.S. participants underscored that a new U.S. administration was unlikely to go out on a limb for peace without substantial pressure to do so. They urged the Colombians to think through carefully what they asked for, and to develop concrete policy proposals that they might help vet and present in Washington.

Participants agreed to discuss the issues raised with their constituencies back home and other organizations not represented at the meeting in Washington. Some of the participants offered to put together a policy brief for the new administration, noting that the Summit of the Americas in April 2009 in Trinidad and Tobago would provide timely opportunities for presenting proposals to the Obama administration and neighboring governments. At the end of the event, there was a call for the organizers to host a second conference in one year's time.

Following the conference, USIP sent out an online survey, to which twenty-one of the sixty-two participants (about 30 percent) responded. The survey assessed the successes and shortcomings of the conference, its relevance for the participants' work, recommendations for follow-up activities, and ways to improve the process.

Respondents appreciated the opportunity the conference offered to bring people together from different organizations and backgrounds, and to build coalitions and make new contacts. Frustration was nonetheless clear over the lack of participation from the Obama transition team, and participants did not have a clear idea about how the ideas discussed in the conference would get to the desk of Obama or other influential government representatives. There was an overall feeling that though the meeting allowed for the discussion of new and innovative ideas, no real action plan was developed. A few participants suggested that working in small groups might have been a helpful way to generate further discussion, interaction, and follow-up activities. Others suggested that greater preparatory work by the civil society leaders, including the elaboration of a policy paper before the meeting, might have helped focus the discussion more. Respondents concurred that one day was too little for an agenda that included both brainstorming and the development of proposals, and that a two- to three-day program would be more productive. Although most of the respondents felt that the selection of the participants was satisfactory, some raised pointed concerns about the representation of ethnic minorities, the need to bring in more regional actors, and the absence of the Colombian government and the Colombian Conference of Bishops, the latter of which had played a key role in virtually all of the prior peace accords. These evaluations provided useful guidance for subsequent stages of the process. CODHES followed up with briefings to some of the sectors that had been absent.

In late January 2009, several weeks after the conference, a facilitated working lunch was convened in Bogotá with about forty of the Colombia-based conference participants and representatives of some of the sectors that had been unable to attend the Washington meeting. The group, which now called itself the Washington Group, related that they had continued to meet and strategize, and were consulting with their constituencies about a proposed letter to President Obama.

The Colombian magazine *Cambio*, reporting on the formation of the Washington Group, announced, "The idea of dialogue with the FARC has little support in Colombia, but is growing abroad."[5] The Asamblea Permanente de la Sociedad Civil por la Paz (Permanent Assembly of Civil Society for Peace), a coalition that included many of the Washington Group members, took out a full-page spread in a Medellín daily, with pictures of the conference in Washington, calling on the international community to support peace in Colombia and outlining some of the initiatives under way.[6] In the following weeks, the group developed its proposals, and further consultations resulted in a letter to President Obama signed by leaders of more than a hundred Colombian civil society organizations representing human rights organizations, academics, labor leaders, jurists, indigenous organizations, women's groups, church leaders (including the Catholic Bishops' Conference), politicians, cultural organizations, and peace organizations.[7] The letter outlined five proposed changes in U.S. policy that would help pave the way for peace in Colombia. It called on the Obama administration to review and revise U.S. drug policy; to encourage a political, negotiated solution to the conflict; to support the independence and strengthening of Colombia's judicial branch; to give priority to human rights as a cornerstone of U.S. policy; and to support a fair and just free trade agreement that protected human rights and did not exacerbate the armed conflict. Representatives of the group presented the letter to the U.S. ambassador in Bogotá.

The Washington Group increasingly took on a life of its own. The discussions of the group nourished a flurry of other activities and collaborations. The Colombians released a document of policy points for the Summit of the Americas held in Trinidad and Tobago in mid-April 2009. A few of the group's members attended the Summit, where they presented their ideas to Latin American government officials. The Permanent Assembly of Civil Society for Peace sent a letter to Chilean president Michelle Bachelet, in her

---

5. "Idea de dialogar con las Farc tiene poca acogida en Colombia, pero se fortalece en el exterior," *Cambio*, January 30, 2009.

6. "La paz en Colombia es posible, con el apoyo de la comunidad internacional," *El Espectador*, Medellin, December 30, 2009, 7.

7. Washington Group, Letter to Barack Obama, n.d., http://www.usip.org/files/Colombia/Colombia%20Web%20Update%206_2011/Letter%20to%20Obama.pdf.

capacity as president pro tempore of the Union of South American Nations (UNASUR), that referenced the Washington Group's letter to President Obama and called on UNASUR to form a Group of Friends and to offer its good offices to overcome the internal armed conflict in Colombia.[8]

Phase Two: Grupo Washington

Meanwhile, the Washington Group continued to meet in Bogotá and stayed in touch by occasional telephone and Skype calls. Preparations began for the second gathering in Washington, which would involve a subset of the Colombians of the Washington Group and take place the first week of December 2009. The organizers sought participation of the members most able to speak directly to the issues outlined in the letter sent to Obama earlier in the year. The delegation included three representatives of the Asamblea Permanente de la Sociedad Civil por la Paz (an umbrella for various peace organizations), which helped finance the delegation; and representatives from Fundación Nuevo Arco Iris, Indepaz, and Planeta Paz. All of the delegates represented peace organizations based in Bogotá, but with offices in other regions as well. Two of the seven delegates were women, one of whom represented Ruta Pacífica, one of Colombia's strongest national women's organizations. None of the regions or ethnic groups was directly represented, nor were the churches or the business community.

The December 2009 program was shaped by the political context in which it occurred. The United States and Colombia had signed a bilateral military agreement on October 30, 2009, that (it was later determined) violated constitutional norms. In response, Venezuela had broken off relations with Colombia and sent troops to its Colombian border. President Uribe, after changing the constitution to run for re-election four years earlier, was setting himself up to run for election yet again. In addition to indictments against more than a third of the national Congress, the para-political scandal now implicated more than a dozen governors, 166 mayors, thirteen deputies, and fifty-eight councilmen. Finally, in the United States, the assistant secretary of state for Latin America had assumed office only three weeks earlier, after an eleven-month delay in his Senate confirmation hearings.

Responding to concerns over the lack of interlocution with the administration the year earlier, for this second meeting in Washington, USIP organized a closed roundtable with the administration, sought and secured a

---

8. Letter to UNASUR, August 5, 2009, Bogotá, reproduced in Asamblea Permanente de la Sociedad Civil por la Paz, *Diplomacia ciudadana por la paz de Colombia*, November 2009, 17–19.

private meeting with the newly arrived assistant secretary for Latin America, and arranged opportunities for private meetings on the Hill, including a briefing for congressional aides hosted by the office of Congressman Sam Farr, a former Peace Corps volunteer who had served in Colombia.

When the Washington Group members arrived from Colombia, CCHR again received them and organized the hospitality. USIP hosted an initial meeting of the delegation, the organizers, and a few local key Colombia analysts. There was some frustration that there had been no answer from the group's letter to President Obama, and one of the goals Colombian civil society leaders laid out for this visit was to secure a response. The last-minute cancellation of the meeting with the assistant secretary of state due to breaking events in Honduras forced a rethinking of their strategy, and the group decided to follow up with the U.S. ambassador in Bogotá on their return.

Two members of the Colombian delegation shared draft concept papers they had developed. The first took stock of the progress on the five topics addressed in the Obama letter. The paper praised Obama's proposal to form an equal partnership with the countries of Latin America, to close Guantánamo, and to prohibit the use of torture. It urged the administration to privilege dialogue and diplomacy over military action in Colombia, and criticized the bilateral military agreement as contradictory to Obama's expressed commitment to that approach. Finally, it proposed a dialogue with Colombian civil society and the new administration.

The second paper envisioned how a multisector, multilateral dialogue could serve as the basis for a new U.S.-Colombia alliance that would support democracy, equity, and sovereignty as the basis for development and security; redefine U.S. aid in favor of the rule of law and peace; and replace the military approach of the prior U.S. administration with an integrated human development approach that assumed co-responsibility of the parties. The delegation discussed both papers and used them as talking points for meetings in Washington and New York.

The roundtable in Washington took place at USIP offices on December 1, 2009. It was a closed meeting designed to enable U.S. policymakers to engage with some of Colombia's leading peace leaders and provide a space for discussing how the United States might more effectively support peace in Colombia and in the region. It was also an opportunity for civil society leaders to ascertain whether U.S. policy toward Colombia could be expected to change with a new administration in Washington.

In the end, the roundtable included twenty-some participants and was divided fairly evenly between representatives of the U.S. government, Colombian NGOs, and U.S. NGOs. A senior administration spokesperson led off with a brief presentation of the administration's assessment of the shifts in the Andean region—the increased participation of previously disenfranchised groups in the political system and the rise of charismatic leaders in Venezuela, Ecuador, and Peru; the search for constructive U.S. engagement in the region; and concerns about the changing nature of the illegal armed actors in Colombia and how such shifts might impact the prospects for a peace process.

Two of the Colombian delegates followed with formal presentations on behalf of the group, outlining their concerns about the military base agreement and its implications for peace and democracy in Colombia and in the region. The first presenter noted that the agreement was reached in secret, without proper consultation with or approval by the Colombian Congress. He underscored the potential negative impact of the agreement on civil-military relations and human rights within Colombia, on relations of the United States and Colombia with the rest of the hemisphere, and on the security of the region as a whole. By shifting the balance of power in the Andes, the accord threatened to unleash a new arms race and to further militarize the region. He urged the U.S. government to reconsider the terms of the accord, which among other things also granted immunity to U.S. soldiers for crimes committed in Colombia, and to respect the judicial processes under way in Colombia to challenge the constitutionality of the agreement.

The second presentation evaluated the successes and shortcomings of the democratic security policy of President Uribe and concluded that, despite some initial successes, the policy's military approach had reached its limit and not brought the country any closer to peace. Paramilitary activity was still pervasive throughout the country; the FARC remained strong militarily, logistically, and numerically; and the ELN was re-emerging. Furthermore, the Colombian military itself was in crisis and facing enormous problems of command-and-control, criminal infiltration, and demoralization as a result of revelations about engagement of its ranks in extrajudicial executions of peasants.

In the exchange that followed, roundtable participants shared their concerns about human rights and peace. They discussed the false positive cases, the emergence of criminal bands, the worrisome rise in guerrilla recruitments of youth and indigenous peoples, the difficult access that Afro-Colombians had to Colombian authorities, the growing numbers of Colombians being displaced by the conflict, the impact of the conflict on women, and the recent extraditions of paramilitary leaders to the United States. The Colombians expressed their concerns about the growing regionalization of the conflict and urged the U.S. government to pressure its Colombian counterparts for a peace process.

U.S. government officials present questioned what the role of the U.S. government might be. They supported a peace process in principle, but were reticent about whether the time was ripe for talks, given that they saw little interest in dialogue on the part of the FARC or ELN. Beyond seeking a negotiated solution with the FARC, the Colombians asserted that the U.S. government could support peace by helping to build and strengthen democratic institutions, root out political corruption, and strengthen the judicial system. They urged the new administration to use its influence to promote human rights and land reform, and to publicly reach out to human rights defenders. They recommended that any future peace process not be limited to a discussion between Colombia's various armed groups but that the Colombian government be encouraged to create and use channels (such as the National Peace Council) for civil society to contribute to the process.

Following the roundtable, CODHES, CCHR, and USIP hosted a working session with Colombian and U.S. civil society leaders that took stock of the process begun in the previous year's meeting and proposed and discussed strategies for moving forward. Consensus was reached that the group should produce policy papers on a small number of priority issues that could be presented in the next year.

The delegation also participated in a congressional briefing, and met with European diplomats, the Colombian ambassador, the Organization of American States, the United Nations, academics, and Colombians living in the greater Washington and New York metropolitan areas.

Formal evaluation of the 2009 activities was conducted in a meeting a few months later in Bogotá and in consultation with several of the participants. Assessments of the dialogue with the U.S. government were mixed. Many of the participants felt that the roundtable had given them a better sense of the possibilities for policy changes under the Obama administration with respect to peace in Colombia, and the role that the Washington Group might play in this regard. The group was disappointed that it had not been able to bring its peace agenda to the attention of Assistant Secretary of State Arturo Valenzuela more directly, and that key sectors of the government—particularly the military and judicial branch—were not present at the roundtable, though they had been invited and in some cases had confirmed their participation. Finally, the group continued to raise concerns about the lack of representation of key sectors of Colombian civil society—business leaders, labor leaders, church, and military—in the dialogues.

A few months later, in March 2010, the Washington Group convened in Bogotá. About thirty Washington Group members, including a few U.S. NGO representatives, attended. Participants assessed the political moment and the status of the different issues that had been identified, and sought to create a common calendar of activities. The agenda had shifted a bit since the first meeting in December 2008. In this session, the group agreed that policy papers should be developed on each of four issues they had identified as being critical to peace—the military base agreement and regional security, human rights and a negotiated settlement, U.S. drug policy, and the Free Trade Agreement. Subgroups were formed and coordinators identified for each theme. The Washington Group made plans to meet in four to six months to review and discuss the draft papers. USIP gave a contract to CODHES to establish a technical secretariat that would convene monthly breakfast meetings of the group, facilitate communications between the North and South, oversee the development of the policy papers, and organize a three-day program in Colombia at which the papers would be presented and discussed.

Phase Three: The Paipa Dialogues

Once again, the dialogue organizers considered the political calendar. Presidential elections were anticipated in Colombia in May, with run-off elections in June and the inauguration of a new president in August. The first semester of 2010 was thus marked by intensive civil society engagement with Colombia's electoral process. The program was scheduled to take place from August 1 through August 3, just days before the newly elected government was to assume power. CODHES booked a retreat center in Paipa, a rural community some three hours outside Bogotá in the department of Boyacá. The accommodations were secure, pleasant, economical, and accessible, but far enough from Bogotá that participants would be inclined to stay for the full three days.

In addition to the opportunities anticipated with a new administration in Bogotá, several unanticipated shifts in the Colombian political scene shaped the Paipa meetings. Only days before the group convened, FARC leader Alfonso Cano issued a video that invited president-elect Juan Manuel Santos to engage in a dialogue for a political solution to the conflict. Also, once again, conflict had intensified with Colombia's neighbors. Accusations by the Colombian ambassador to the Organization of American States that Venezuela was harboring FARC terrorists had prompted troop movements in that country.

With a new administration in Bogotá, a call for dialogue from the guerrillas, and the threat of armed conflict on the borders, the Paipa meetings could not have been more timely. The gathering at Paipa included twenty-nine people, most of who had been in the initial meeting in 2008. New participants included representatives from regions outside of Bogotá, and a few invited experts on drugs and policy issues. U.S. participants included seven representatives of U.S. NGOs.

The dialogues opened on Sunday evening with a welcome reception, a special recognition of the work of one of the North Americans, Adam Isacson, and dinner. CODHES and USIP co-moderated the program, which began the next morning. After a round of introductions and a review of the activities of the Washington Group process, participants were asked to summarize their hopes and expectations for the Paipa meetings. Participants wanted to share analysis of the shifting political contexts in the United States and Colombia, and to identify and strategize about opportunities for action. They wanted to discuss how to legitimize speaking about peace, to discuss the formulation of public peace policies, and to build bridges between local, regional, and national peace initiatives. They hoped the meetings would provide an opportunity for supporting dialogue, coordinating advocacy, and creating a peace agenda for a more comprehensive peace movement. They wanted to develop a structure for continuing to meet, for citizens' diplomacy in the United States, and for putting peace in Colombia on the U.S. agenda.

The program, originally intended to review the draft policy papers and develop a strategy for moving forward, had shifted somewhat to take advantage of the new political moment in Colombia. Commitment by Vice President–elect Angelino Garzón to participate in an opening panel at Paipa had given the meetings a particular sense of timeliness, urgency, and importance; unfortunately, the vice president elect had to cancel his participation at the last minute. The legislative director from the office of Representative James P. McGovern (D-MA), who had accompanied the process from the start, and a Colombian political scientist from the Universidad Nacional launched the first panel discussion on U.S.-Colombian relations. A presentation by one of the Washington Group members followed with a presentation on land issues, a theme not addressed by the group previously but identified as a priority by the incoming Santos administration. The group next watched the video of the FARC leader's call for dialogue, which had just been posted on-line. Participants analyzed the clip and concurred on a welcome shift in tone, content, and proposals that suggested improved prospects for dialogue.[9]

The participants in 2008 had preferred to have all conversations as a ple-nary, but enough trust had now been achieved to vary the format. USIP identified four participants particularly attuned to issues of process, and asked them to serve as facilitators for smaller group works. The facilitators met together over lunch and designed a common methodology for these break-out sessions. When the plenary reconvened, the new methodology was presented and approved. Authors were asked to present their drafts to the plenary, which would then divide into smaller discussion groups. Each of the smaller groups was asked to articulate the message on the particular theme that Colombians and their counterparts wished to convey to U.S. policymakers, the changes they wanted to see, and the steps needed to make the proposals viable. The facilitator helped keep the small groups on task, and each group selected a rapporteur who would report back to the plenary. This process was repeated for each of the four issue areas. After the last round of small group work, the plenary session was used to prioritize the ideas that had emerged and to identify potential follow-up actions related to each theme. Individuals then made commitments on behalf of their organizations to carry out the activities identified.

As with the first gathering in December 2008, USIP organized and dis-tributed an online survey to which twelve of the thirty-three participants (just over 30 percent) responded. Most of the respondents noted that the meetings continued to build international solidarity and important links and networks between U.S. and Colombian civil society organizations. They also identified a number of ways in which the dialogue process could be improved. They called for more advance preparation, including the distribution of rel-evant reports and papers before the events. Participants recommended find-ing ways to incorporate Colombian NGOs and community leaders engaged in exemplary local and regional peacemaking models into the Washington Group process. Concerns were again expressed about the composition of the group, with a call for greater representation from the business sector, indig-enous communities, trade unions, the churches, internally displaced persons, and both the U.S. and Colombian governments.

Some felt that the agenda was too ambitious and that the group needed to focus more on how the topics selected related to the central issues of peace

9.   Virginia M. Bouvier, "Cautious Optimism for Peace in Colombia," USIP Peace Brief, September 2010, http://www.usip.org/publications/cautious-optimism-peace-in-colombia.

and human rights. Participants expressed their hope for follow-through on the agendas, proposals, and commitments that came out of the conference, and urged that a conference report be produced and circulated. A number of ideas and projects—including an online mechanism to facilitate the sharing of ideas, information, analysis, proposals, and joint initiatives—were proposed, but most felt that it would be prudent to see what the first few months of the Santos administration would bring, and to assess the attitude of the Obama administration toward Colombia given the change in Colombian leadership.

Outcomes

It is too early to evaluate fully the impact of the dialogues but nonetheless clear that they have created and strengthened sustainable relationships between the participants and helped build capacity among civil society leaders in Colombia and the United States for peacemaking and peacebuilding.

Renewed optimism about the potential for a political solution to the Colombian conflict is evident in a variety of developments:

- enhanced understanding of U.S. government institutions and advocacy,
- new opportunities for sharing information,
- new and stronger working relationships and alliances within Colombia,
- heightened trust and contact between groups in the United States and Colombia,
- more personal contacts and joint projects,
- Colombian participants eager to serve as interlocutors,
- improved U.S. policymaker access to Colombia's leading peace proponents, and
- new relationships with the international community.

After nearly three years, the dialogues have helped focus conversations within Colombian civil society around a national peace agenda. They have brought differences among the participants to the surface and explore the nature of civil society's participation in a peace process, how to create an environment propitious for peace, and what should be asked of the international community.

Lessons Learned

Several elements of the civil society dialogues appear to have been particularly successful.

- First, the process was driven by the Colombians rather than the facilitators. USIP worked with and at the behest of a Colombian partner who was able to identify and engage key participants themselves highly motivated to engage in a common process.
- Second, USIP had a D.C.-based partner whose initiative and ideas helped shape the initial conference program that launched the process, and which was able to provide hospitality that increased opportunities for informal exchange.
- Third, consultation was important at every step of the way to help ensure good programs that responded to the needs of the stakeholders in Colombia and had political relevance in a U.S. policy environment. The consultation process itself provided opportunities to put peace on the agenda of policymakers and NGOs, and to encourage reflection on concrete policy options.
- Fourth, there was an occasional clash, given the different personalities, objectives, approaches, and organizational styles and cultures. Negotiating these conflicts required reframing differences as complementary rather than competing. Strong historical ties and relationships between the lead organizers, patience and good humor, and the shared desire for successful events helped smooth these relatively minor bumps.
- Fifth, agility in anticipating or responding to opportunities created by a particular political moment and context was key. The dialogues were well timed to take advantage of perceived windows of opportunity. This gave a focus and a sense of urgency to the gatherings and ensured channels for moving agendas forward.
- Sixth, U.S. and Colombian NGOs that participated in the dialogues were already attuned to policy issues and engaged in high-quality analysis. The programs were designed to take advantage of this intellectual capital and to maximize opportunities to share expertise and to generate new thinking.
- Seventh, the dialogues (increasingly over time) built in sufficient time for networking to help sow the seeds of future collaborations. Travel, meals, social activities, working groups, planning sessions that engaged participants, a comfortable site with meeting spaces for informal exchanges, and follow-up activities that required a process of reaching out and reporting back all provided opportunities to enhance these relationships.
- Eighth, the moderators played a role in ensuring that all those at the table had an equal opportunity to voice their views and concerns, and

that the programmatic structure remained attuned to the mood and needs of the participants.

- Ninth, the iterative nature of the meetings helped strengthen working relationships and built trust both within Colombia and across the North-South divide. With each meeting, the discussions delved a bit deeper, and participants became more willing to vocalize their differences.

- Finally, USIP engaged a plethora of monitoring and evaluation mechanisms—evaluation discussions at the close of each program, formal electronic surveys, follow-up visits and meetings to review progress and take stock of next steps, and informal queries to those inside and outside of the process. These feedback mechanisms have enabled the organizers to improve the design and execution of subsequent stages of the process.

This discussion has already addressed many of the areas that could be improved in relation to each phase, but two final observations are merited. First, the organizers—USIP, CCHR, and CODHES—would have done well to develop a communications strategy that served the needs of the group. Internal communications were inconsistent between events, and there was no apparent strategy for communication with external audiences, for dissemination of written materials that the group produced, or for documentation of such activities. Efforts to regularize communication by creating a technical secretariat following the second meeting in 2009 did not seem to improve the flow of information.

Second, in the field of peacebuilding, the question of who gets to participate in a given process (and in what capacity) is perhaps the most contentious, most revealing, and one of the most important elements of the process. This was certainly the case with the dialogues. Colombia, like many countries in conflict, is a nation divided by class, race and ethnicity, region, gender, age, religion, and ideology. There are sharp fissures between rural and urban areas; between Bogotá and the regions; and between historically poor, displaced individuals and communities and former combatants. Women, the rural sectors in general and the rural poor in particular, youth, Afro-Colombians, and the indigenous have a history of political, social, and economic exclusion in Colombia, and they are also bearing the brunt of the armed conflict. These divisions and differential experiences are expressed starkly in the geography of the armed conflict and they permeate efforts to resolve it. The reproduction of exclusions is not inevitable, and the organizers and participants in the conference were attuned to this issue at every step of the process. The dialogues demonstrated just how difficult it is to get alternative voices to the table. The organizers reviewed the participant lists to ensure diversity among the participants and representation of key sectors, yet they had no control over who would accept the invitations. There was also no mechanism designed to ensure that these sectors had a real voice when they participated. Overcoming historical exclusions required more resources than this project had. Future dialogues should consider formats that involve marginalized groups in the leadership of the process itself, create processes of prior consultation to ensure formats for meaningful participation, or create complementary processes among these groups that identify and address the barriers to their participation.

By way of conclusion, the impact of peacemaking and peacebuilding projects and processes is likely to be cumulative over time. Individual and collective evaluation and reflection can create awareness of the strengths and constraints of the process, allow for needed adjustments, and provide important guidance for shaping future directions that can be increasingly effective. Processes have their own rhythms, and these must be approached with patience and humility.

6

Nigeria: Dialogue in the Delta

Judith Burdin Asuni

Nigeria's Niger Delta is a rich oil-producing region plagued by intense interethnic fighting and, more recently, attacks from armed militants against oil industry and government facilities. It is also the site of two USIP-funded conflict management projects executed between 1999 and 2007 by Academic Associates PeaceWorks (AAPW). The first was a two-year facilitated dialogue among the three ethnic groups involved in long-term competition and conflict near the coastal town of Warri, Delta State. The second project brought together stakeholders from twenty conflict-prone local governments (similar to counties) to work for nonviolent elections in 2007. Thus, over about seven years, AAPW used a model of facilitated dialogue developed in the late 1990s for use in Nigeria's Middle Belt on several land-based ethnic conflicts, modifying it for the more complex Warri conflict.

This chapter tells the stories of a number of people because conflicts involve people and people are the ones who have to solve or manage them.

Background

The Niger Delta encompasses six coastal states, where most of the country's oil and gas are produced: Edo, Delta, Bayelsa, Rivers, Akwa Ibom, and Cross River. Most of the oil-related conflicts happen in three: Delta, Bayelsa, and Rivers. The Warri conflicts have arisen between various combinations of the Itsekiri, Urhobo, and Ijaw ethnic groups over the past fifty years, but reached new heights in 1997 and 1999.

Warri, today a rapidly growing metropolis of more than 500,000 people, was one of the first points of contact between European explorers and what is now Nigeria, which the British colonial government created in 1914 from several autonomous kingdoms. The Portuguese were the first to land near Warri, and a member of the Itsekiri royal family went to study medicine in Portugal in the sixteenth century. Because of their early contact with Europeans and subsequent access to education and Western languages, the Itsekiris often acted as middlemen between the foreigners and other ethnic groups, developing an air of what the Nigerians call overlordship, or superiority. Their immediate neighbors were the Urhobos, who resented advantages given the Itsekiris by colonial powers. In spite of this rivalry, the Itsekiris and Urhobos frequently intermarried and lived together in relative peace. The term *Warri Boy* referred to savvy urban youth of both ethnic groups. A third group, the Ijaws, until the past few decades generally lived in isolated small settlements along the creeks of the Delta, where they were fishermen. When the Ijaws talk of going home they refer to "going to the river."

The peaceful coexistence of Itsekiris, Urhobos, and Ijaws deteriorated with the arrival of the oil industry in the 1990s. The issue of ownership came to the fore, because the oil companies pay rent, give compensation for environmental damage, hire local staff, and award contracts, all based at least in part on their perception of who owns the land on which facilities are located. In law, all land is technically owned by the national government, which also owns all mineral resources. However, across the Niger Delta various ethnic groups or communities compete with each other over this ownership. The companies did not always study the situation carefully before making decisions about who would benefit from oil development. Company staff members with vested interests sometimes exacerbated the problems. Warri has therefore seen violent competition for control of resources and related benefits, as there are a number of companies and facilities in the area. It is also one of the few areas where three different ethnic groups live in such close proximity. A third factor is the existing antagonism resulting from external colonial influence.

After several decades of waxing and waning, conflict in Warri blew up in 1997 with the creation of new local governments, which were seen as rich sources of jobs and revenue. For some inexplicable reason,[1] the headquarters of the Warri Southwest Local Government had been first located by the federal government in an Ijaw area and then moved to an Itsekiri town. The

---

1. Warri was not the only example of decisions that seemed illogical. A similar movement of the local government headquarters in Ife-Modakeke, Osun State, created an equally deadly competition between two sub-ethnic groups. Similarly, manipulation of local government demarcations in Takum, Taraba State, led to a deadly conflict between the Chamba and Kuteb ethnic groups. Selfish interests and political maneuvering are often behind such decisions.

result was fighting between these two groups, with the Urhobos supporting the Ijaw cause. Many villages were burned in the riverine area, and the fighting extended into Warri city. It was particularly fierce in the Okere quarter, where the Itsekiris and Urhobos have both traditionally lived. People moved out of ethnically heterogeneous areas to safer ethnic strongholds. Commerce was at a standstill. A number of companies servicing the oil industry left Warri and moved to Port Harcourt. Political interests with economic repercussions compounded long-standing ethnic mistrust and competition for control of oil facilities.

The Process

AAPW applied to USIP for a grant to work on the Warri conflict. Awarded in early 1999, research was to begin that summer. In retrospect the proposal was far too ambitious, especially for a budget of $45,000. It included the following elements:

- a case study,
- case study analysis and training of mediators,
- training of youth leaders,
- training of community leaders,
- conciliation visits,
- follow-up visits,
- a Warri peace forum,
- enlightenment visits, and
- publication of a book.

Additional grants from the United States Agency for International Development/Office of Transition Initiatives (USAID/OTI) extended the duration and scope of work in the Warri area, which made follow-up much easier and incorporated participants from the USIP-sponsored events, thus reinforcing learning and behavioral change. The first such grant was for peace education training for secondary school teachers in Warri in December 1999. A second grant was awarded to conduct conflict management training for local government officials, youth leaders, and elders in fifteen local governments in the three core Niger Delta states—Delta, Bayelsa and Rivers—between December 1999 and April 2000. This combination of many activities reinforced each other and created a high level of awareness of peacebuilding work in the Warri area. The involvement of a number of high-profile civil society leaders and members of the state government peace process permitted access to top state government and security officials as well as to the media.

The plan for the Warri intervention evolved out of ongoing work by AAPW in other Nigerian conflicts. It was designed by a heterogeneous network of AAPW staff, academics, a retired army general, and grassroots practitioners.

AAPW Experience

A Nigerian NGO, AAPW was founded in 1988 and became active in conflict management activities in the early 1990s, when this was a new field virtually unknown in Nigeria. It began with volunteers conducting peace education programs in primary and secondary schools. In the absence of donor funding, AAPW approached General Olusegun Obasanjo, a former military chief of state, and together organized a first workshop in 1993 for university staff and students, hosted by Obasanjo's Africa Leadership Forum with a guest facilitator, Richard Salem of Conflict Management Initiatives in Evanston, Illinois. Over breakfast on the general's rooftop one morning, the idea was conceived of a National Corps of Mediators—senior Nigerians trained to intervene in communal conflict. Salem returned the following year for the launch of this corps. This work was funded by the Africa Leadership Forum and largely facilitated by AAPW without compensation. The National Corps of Mediators' first intervention was in Jos in April 1994 between Christian indigenes and Muslim settlers.

When Obasanjo was imprisoned the following year, the Corps went into dormancy until 1995, when the British Council developed an interest in conflict management and began funding the work of AAPW. Along with a small peace NGO in Kaduna, AAPW organized conflict management workshops across Nigeria funded by the British Council and later the UK Department for International Development (DFID), with emphasis on interreligious and interethnic conflict. One year money was left over, which the British Council agreed to devote to case studies on a number of communal conflicts. These were included in a book, *Community Conflicts in Nigeria: Management, Resolution and Transformation*,[2] first published in 1999 and reprinted twice.

These case studies set the course for future work: to transform a conflict, the underlying causes and key actors had to be identified. Moving on from

---

2. Onigu Otite and Isaac Olawale Albert, *Community Conflicts in Nigeria: Management, Resolution and Transformation* (Ibadan: Spectrum Press, 1999).

the original three-day workshops, more sustained two-year interventions into specific community conflicts were launched, again with British Council/DFID support. The first such interventions were in Zangon Kataf in Kaduna State, where Kataf Christian indigenes and Muslim Hausa settlers were fighting for control, as well as Tafawa Balewa in Bauchi State, where Sayawa Christian indigenes and Muslim Hausa settlers were in dispute. Later, two-year interventions were undertaken in several other communities with funding from USAID.

The AAPW team members had varied backgrounds. One research and intervention officer, Shedrack Best, had a PhD from Bradford in peace studies and later became the head of the peace studies program at the University of Jos. The other, Isaac Albert, was sent by the British Council to do peace studies at Bradford and subsequently established a peace studies program at the University of Ibadan. The adviser, Major-General Ishola Williams (retired) had peacekeeping and strategic studies experience from his days in the Nigerian Army. Some of the younger staff members were sent for training at Responding to Conflict in Birmingham, UK; the Centre for Conflict Resolution in Cape Town, South Africa; and Eastern Mennonite University in Virginia, USA.

Despite having no formal training in conflict management, Judith Asuni had a PhD in sociology and had accompanied a mentor, Richard Salem, during his visits to Nigeria. Asuni had also attended short courses at CCR, Responding to Conflict, and INCORE in Londonderry, Northern Ireland, and had visited peacebuilding centers in the United States as well as peace organizations in Ireland. She thus had few theoretical preconceptions about how conflicts should be managed but a burning desire to make people aware that conflicts can indeed be resolved, to build their capacities to do so, and to provide the information and training required. These became the objectives of AAPW and its activities, including the Warri intervention.

As the first NGO to work widely on community conflicts in Nigeria, the AAPW team members learned on their feet and developed new strategies and foci as necessary. Over time, they moved more into combining peacebuilding and conflict-sensitive development, especially in a multifaceted approach used in Karu (near Abuja) and in a MacArthur Foundation project in the Niger Delta. AAPW also adopted stakeholder partnering, working with various partners: government at the federal, state, and local levels, oil and gas companies, the security agencies, foreign donors, and Nigerian communities.

The Warri Effort

Beginning the work on Warri, AAPW brought in two respected and neutral academics to coordinate research, Thomas Imobighe[3] of Ambrose Alli University in Edo State, and Celestine Bassey, an indigene of Cross River State but teaching at Delta State University in 1999. AAPW hosted a first meeting of the research team, which also included Ijaw, Urhobo, and Itsekiri scholars, in Benin City (in neighboring Edo State) in early May 1999.

Violence broke out again shortly thereafter, only a few days after the inauguration of the new state government on May 29, 1999, and subsequent government peace efforts understandably aimed for quick results.[4] This well-intentioned initiative was premature, however, and entrenched the already intransigent positions of the various sides, something that had occurred also in previous government efforts. It also set up a parallel effort to AAPW's, one in which participants were paid "sitting allowances" that AAPW, for reasons of both budget and principle, did not provide. The government initiative bypassed the kind of dialogue process which AAPW had in mind, which aims at deep listening, shared inquiry, and shared meaning-making.[5]

Thus, by the time that AAPW began its dialogue process in October 1999, deal-making was already under way, with none of the prerequisite listening, inquiry, or cooperative effort. This situation was quite different from that envisioned more than a year earlier in the proposal to USIP. It required considerable effort to go back to the stage of listening to each other and developing a shared vision. This was eventually achieved but would have been easier without the violence of May and June, followed by premature negotiations.

In addition, the violence made it impossible for the interethnic team members to stay together or even to leave their own ethnic areas. The two research coordinators therefore had to move among the three research teams. The heightened tension also made it difficult for the local researchers to maintain their intellectual neutrality, so each ethnic group was interviewed separately. The situation would continue to change over the subsequent two-year effort. Fortunately, the USIP grant was supplemented with funds from USAID/OTI between 1999 and 2001, and from the U.S. embassy in Abuja

---

3. Imobighe was a Jennings Randolph Senior Fellow at USIP.

4. Renewed interethnic violence around the 2003 elections showed that the quick fix didn't work.

5. Bettye Pruitt and Philip Thomas, "Democratic Dialogue: A Handbook for Practitioners" (Washington, DC: General Secretariat of the Organization of American States; Stockholm: International Institute for Democracy and Electoral Assistance; New York: United Nations Development Programme, 2007), 23, figure 1.3.1.

and from Chevron in 2003. The various funding sources did not place conflicting demands on AAPW, and the additional funding enabled AAPW to undertake work on addressing renewed political violence.

Participants, Facilitators, and Staff

For the people of Warri to own the peace process, it had to be led by some of their own. Where could six people from the three different ethnic groups safely meet in a strife-torn city? Luckily, a large Petroleum Training Institute in Effurun on the outskirts of Warri is viewed as neutral territory. Its conference center became the team's base of activity for the next few years.

Participants were selected on the basis of being a "microcosm of the system that creates problems and who have to be part of the solution."[6] The obvious candidates in this case were the three ethnic groups who were fighting each other: Itsekiris, Urhobos, and Ijaws. The less obvious players were others who helped to create problems—the political class, the security agencies, the oil companies, other ethnic groups within Delta State, Deltans in the diaspora, and other parties within Nigeria. It is often difficult to dissect the motives of such groups. For example, not long into our peace process, a group was formed called the 3I's Forum. This consisted of representatives of the Ijaws, Itsekiris, and Isokos (the last a neighboring ethnic group not directly involved in the Warri conflict). The Urhobos were not included in this group, which generated resentment. This forum was theoretically set up to bring peace and development to the area. In reality, it was a political forum of the three smaller ethnic groups in Delta South senatorial district[7] who were trying to wrest political power away from the Urhobos, the largest ethnic group in Delta State. This forum confused the scene for some time and reinforced suspicions and resentments within the three ethnic groups actually residing in Warri.

The AAPW intervention of 1999 through 2001 did not include a number of the conflict creators. Recognizing the unexpected consequences of a limited definition of *inclusion*, participation was later expanded.

By October 1999, the research interviews had produced a case study that laid out the factual basis of the Warri conflict in a neutral and analytical way. Based on the work of the research teams, two respected and moder-

---

6. Pruitt and Thomas, "Democratic Dialog," 25.

7. Each state in Nigeria is divided into three senatorial districts, each with one senator in the National Assembly. Theoretically, certain political positions, such as the governorship, rotate among the senatorial districts.

ate members of each ethnic group were identified as facilitators for the intervention.[8] All key opinion leaders in their respective communities, they were invited to review the presented facts and agree on the situation as it was and what it could become. After three days of heated discussion of feelings and experiences, the six managed to reach consensus on what they called "our shared vision."

One Itsekiri facilitator was Chief Dr. Mrs. P. E. B. Uku, a member of the National Corps of Mediators. Well respected, well connected, and urbane, she had earlier engaged in a heated argument with an Ijaw childhood friend, former UN ambassador B. A. Clark,[9] during a role play of the Warri conflict. Even the most sophisticated find it hard to overcome primordial loyalties when the stakes are high. This emotional investment was also demonstrated by the other Itsekiri mediator, Eni Jones Umuko, a university lecturer in theater, who was also a member of the state government peace committee. At one point during the initial workshop, Eni became so emotionally engaged that he shouted at some of the other ethnic leaders. Later, distraught over his behavior, he publicly apologized to the group, which set a good tone for admission of mistakes and forgiveness.

The team also inherited an Urhobo facilitator, Wilson Eboh, from the government peace committee. Another man had initially been identified to become part of the process but during the October meeting of the facilitators, Eboh and Chief W. A. Digbori insisted that the recommended member could not be included, because he was from a neighboring town and not Warri. That individual graciously withdrew and Eboh joined the team. Eboh is a broadcaster from the Okere Urhobo kingdom; Digbori is a retired civil servant from the Agbarha kingdom. The two Urhobos thus represented each kingdom within Warri town.

One of the Ijaw mediators was also part of the government peace committee, Chief E. E. Ebimami, a retired banker. The second Ijaw was the Reverend Professor C. A. Dime, a university professor from the university in Ekpoma, Edo State, and respected as the first president of the Ijaw National Congress, but the distance between his university and Warri reduced his role in the activities. Neither of the Ijaws were from Warri town itself, but that did not matter to the Ijaws.

---

8. The Nigerian definition of *mediator* can vary. For example, in the USIP work in the Wukari conflict, a former deputy governor was definitely more of an arbitrator than a mediator, but the local people in Warri were more facilitators than mediators.

9. He is also the brother of author J. P. Clark and of Chief E. K. Clark, the self-declared National Ijaw leader who has a strong role in the Goodluck Jonathan administration.

Despite a bumpy ride, over time Uku and Ebimami carried the process along, both by the force of their personalities and by their status in the community. The first meeting of the facilitators, in October 1999, was emotionally heated. By the end of three days, however, they had reached a working understanding. Over the next two years, suspicions reared their ugly heads periodically. At one point, Uku, who was carrying the brunt of the work, suspected Ebimami of having sold out by accepting money from the government, though in fact he had gone underground after threats to his life. It took days of telephone calls to reestablish trust between the two. Eboh was also threatened several times and one point kidnapped by Ijaw youths in the course of his duties as the land secretary for the Okere Urhobo kingdom. A well-placed telephone call to the Ijaw youth secured his release.

Over the years, the facilitators and staff came to work as a team. Several of the facilitators participated in other AAPW activities, including peace education and local government workshops. Ebimami even went to Rivers State to facilitate in some of the local governments there. The three key mediators— Uku, Ebimami, and Eboh—became especially close, attending the launch of a community conflicts book in Lagos in March 2000, participating in a conflict management forum hosted by President Obasanjo in Abuja in February 2001, and attending the marriage of the author's daughter in January 2007.

After the initial training, much of the facilitation responsibility was turned over to these six. The analytical aspects of the intervention were handled by the two case study coordinators, Imobighe and Bassey. Both understandably tended to lecture to the participants. The experiential aspects of the workshops were handled by Ralph Ekeh and Patterson Ogon. Ralph at that time was a tall, slim Igbo in his twenties and an excellent facilitator and trainer. At the beginning of the facilitators' training, most wondered what this young man had to offer. By the end, they affectionately called him "our teacher." Patterson Ogon, a young Ijaw human rights activist, served as second trainer. Judith Asuni handled overall coordination, problem solving, and public relations.

Previous AAPW interventions had determined it best to start with the youth, because they are the ones whose lives are destroyed—physically, socially, or financially—by armed conflict. If the youth stop fighting, the fighting stops. The mediators therefore identified ten youth leaders from each of the three ethnic groups. Those selected attended a workshop in early November 1999. The mediators also identified ten adult leaders from the three groups, who had their own workshop later the same month. From the case study and analysis during the mediators' training, it appears that this effort reached the real actors in the conflict. Local government chairmen and state government officials also participated. Other activities in the Warri area not directly funded by USIP included peace education for secondary schools and training of local government officials. Again, selection was carefully made on the basis of ethnicity, age, gender, and social organizational ties.

The Dialogue

The dialogue process began with a thorough case study that identified both issues in the conflict and also key actors. The six mediators were identified and came together from October 27 through October 29, 1999. Training in conflict management came first, a sound and nonthreatening basis on which to establish trust and cooperation before getting to the meat of the conflict. It was followed by analysis of the case study, in which all facilitators expressed their perceptions and assumptions. Too often discussions of the Warri conflict have stopped at discussion of the problem and included no real attempt to look for solutions. The mediators pressed ahead for a common vision they had jointly developed—"Our Land"—emphasizing the commonalities of all being part of Warri rather than fighting over origin or ownership.

The facilitators were then assigned the task of choosing ten youth leaders from their respective ethnic groups to come to a workshop in a quiet village far away from Warri from November 10 through November 12, 1999. The case study made it clear that the leaders chosen were the real belligerents in the conflict. This was the first time that the youth had met face to face since the May violence, and for many since 1997, when they had been on opposite sides of the fighting lines. The groups came separately and initially slept and ate separately.

That arrangement changed when the workshop started. AAPW had developed a technique, Sharing Our Stories, in which pairs from opposing sides introduce each other. It is effective, evocative, and powerful to see heads of opposing groups stand up together, introduce each other, remember old alliances and often end up with their arms around each other's shoulders. The same thing happened at this event. Warri Boys is an identity common to all the ethnic groups.

The first night included four hours of listening to each participant tell his experiences during the conflict. This is useful, because the various sides seldom understand how the others feel or what they have gone through. It also underscores commonalities—suffering, death, loss, desire for it to be over.

The next morning began with basic training in conflict management, then went on to analyzing the Warri conflict, in ethnically heterogeneous small working groups. Predictably, the groups' reports were similar. However, for the first time in seven years of conflict management work all across Nigeria, the working groups could not agree on solutions. AAPW had worked in some extremely violent conflicts, but this workshop was also the first time that participants came close to resuming the physical fight during our meeting. The facilitators had earlier asked about security arrangements and been told that each pair was responsible for its ten youth leaders. The workshop proceeded calmly until the last session, in which the group was trying to determine solutions. Bassey and Ebimami were facilitating the session. Voices were raised. People began shouting. Fists were raised. The facilitators were forced to enter the fray and told everyone firmly to sit down. Most did, though a few remained on their feet shouting. These few were told that they would have to leave the venue if they did not sit down. Finally, after a stare-down, everyone sat down to a discussion of how such behavior could cause a resurgence of the crisis. Was that what they wanted? No, they responded. Discussion then moved forward to how to prevent the crisis from returning. This broke the logjam and led into an action plan.

This event demonstrates three things critical to facilitation: being continuously attuned to subtle clues of group dynamics and the environment,[10] having experienced facilitators with a certain force of personality and presence to command the respect of participants, and bringing the process back on track if it starts to derail.

The next step was a similar workshop held on November 24 and 25, 1999, for thirty elders, again selected by the mediators. Ten of the youth asked to come to talk with their elders about the urgency of stopping the conflict. The speeches by youth representatives of the three different ethnic groups were moving and set a positive tone for the workshop, which followed a similar pattern to the earlier one. This time the elders were able to agree on some common grounds. With both the youth and the elders, the facilitators emphasized the idea of "Warri—our land." This was most effective because it came from them. This is also one of the goals of dialogue, to achieve a new shared meaning that the participants create and own.

---

10. Once while facilitating a workshop in Anyama, Bayelsa State (an area where a neighboring community had recently been destroyed), unknown youth circled the venue in increasing numbers and tipped off AAPW that it was about to be attacked. A young Ijaw staff member was sent out to meet with them and diffuse the situation. In a meeting on reflecting on peace practice, another Ijaw woman told the story of the youth leader of one group being kidnapped by the opposing group right in her workshop. This emphasizes the facilitator's responsibility to keep participants safe.

Over time, the Warri peace process evolved in ways not envisioned, re-sponding to needs as they arose. The youth decided to establish a Warri Peace Forum, to resume attending other groups' sports events and cultural festivals (such interaction had ceased during the crisis), and to organize joint rallies, with the host group providing security for the others. The elders set up an interethnic committee. They also pressured the government to reha-bilitate destroyed areas and the oil companies to hire more ethnically diverse employees. AAPW met with the local government chairmen in the Warri area and eventually with the Delta State officials, including the governor. The team of facilitators also met with President Obasanjo to brief him on the situation in Warri.

AAPW kept in regular touch with the mediators, key youth, and adult leaders through regular visits to Warri and telephone calls. The facilita-tors made conciliation efforts, initially within their own ethnic groups, but eventually across ethnic lines. The big proposed Warri Peace Forum could not be held until mid-November 2000, a full year after the initial training. This delay, however, gave the participants the opportunity to assess what had unfolded in the interim. The forum demonstrated the need to take messages of peace to the outlying areas, where much of the destruction had happened and where feelings were still high. These areas tend to have pockets of Itsekiri villages or Ijaw villages. Uku and Ebimami volunteered to tour the riverine areas together, traveling in an open speedboat, preach-ing peace together.

The USIP grant ended in March 2001. AAPW approached Delta State governor James Ibori for further funding. However, as so often happens, once peace is established, priorities shift, and few are concerned about main-taining the peace. Serious interethnic conflict in Warri arose again in 2003, this time in response to the national elections. In mid-2003, AAPW was approached by the U.S. embassy and Chevron (which had been negatively affected by the crisis) about resuming peace efforts. Imobighe was again in-volved. By this time, AAPW had also established good political connections at the federal and state levels, so the chief of army staff, minister of state for petroleum (who is from Warri), representatives of the navy, state security services, and the newly established Joint Task Force (JTF) were part of the dialogue. The secretary to the state government (SSG), Emmanuel Udu-aghan (now Delta State governor), participated in the first dialogue. Meet-ings continued for some months until tensions had reduced.

The presence of many other actors in the conflict in this peace process went far toward making it successful and sustainable. It also provided both a useful list of contacts in the region and ongoing regular cooperation with the JTF for several years, the SSG during 2006 and 2007, and Dr. Uduaghan on a proactive strategy for peace and security after he was elected governor in April 2007.

Including a variety of actors informed the AAPW's composition of non-violent election committees (NECs), with funding from USIP, during the 2007 elections. AAPW received a large grant from DFID to support Niger Delta youth working for nonviolent elections, which included rallies, town hall meetings, voter education, election observation, and work on postelection conflict. These two grants also dovetailed into an early warning system funded by the Nigerian National Petroleum Corporation. The NECs were established in twenty of the most conflict-prone local governments in the three core states of the Niger Delta and were facilitated by master trainers, often ex-militants. The committees included representatives of the Independent Electoral Commission, five political parties, the police, state security services, traditional rulers, local government officials, companies present in the area, women, youth, male community leaders, and NGOs. These NECs often dealt with cult or communal conflicts as well as with those related to elections. Perceptions of the young master trainers changed as they moved away from violence toward constructive engagement. By having a variety of actors in the NECs, AAPW was able to handle more causes of conflict as well as more possible solutions.

Outcomes

By late January 2011, a number of companies that had moved out to Port Harcourt or Lagos during the 1997–99 period were moving back. The port was bustling once again. A significant interethnic disagreement in the past had been the use of the term the "Olu of Warri." The Urhobos and Ijaws had greatly resented the Itsekiri king being recognized as the king of the entire town and insisted that he be referred to as the "Olu of Itsekiri." Although still called that by the Itsekiri, other ethnic groups call him simply "the Olu" and recognize him as an important traditional ruler. Ethnicity is no longer uppermost in everyone's mind. The Warri Boys are back.

How much of this can be attributed to AAPW's facilitated dialogue? As in any peace process, it is hard to say. The AAPW team was the first to facilitate a real dialogue among the warring parties after the 1999 violence and again after the 2003 conflict. Other efforts were also made, however. The Delta State government made some of the youth leaders special assistants or commissioners and eventually also set up a ministry of Peace and Conflict Resolution, which undertook reconciliation efforts. In 2003, the head of this ministry refused to work with AAPW. In 2007, however, the new governor encouraged him to collaborate with AAPW peace and development efforts. How much of this is synergy and how much is simply the passage of time? Or is it diversion of attention to other interests, such as politics?

The intervention did seem to have a genuine impact on some of the participants, especially the youth. Often the youth are looking for another way of doing things, or a way out of violence, but don't know how to do it until someone shows them. Like other mentoring relationships, the impact is long lasting.

Lessons Learned

AAPW learned that it is necessary to involve all actors—positive and negative, direct and indirect—in any peace process and has tried to implement this in more recent interventions.

It is also essential, if peace is to be sustainable, that the government be involved.[11] In the late 1990s, AAPW worked in several interethnic conflicts. The governor of Kaduna State addressed a fundamental grievance in Zango Kataf and the conflict has not recurred. The successive governors of Bauchi State have not taken such action in Tafawa Balewa and the conflict recurred as recently as January 2011. It is often difficult to get the government involved in purely civil society activities, but highly placed people, such as our Warri chiefs, can usually help build cooperation.

Peace processes, it is now recognized, often take a decade to consolidate. Too often, civil society groups or even governments undertake one workshop or meeting, or extend their efforts perhaps one or two years at best. For issues to be addressed, consensus to be built, and sustainable results to be achieved, facilitated efforts must be sustained. This is not easy when civil society organizations have to rely on grants, especially when donors change priorities, and conflicts or differences do not necessarily follow these priorities.

Parties to conflicts also often have a vested interest in keeping the conflict going. The AAPW peace efforts in the Niger Delta, for example, were a threat to and often thwarted by people in power—whether politicians, military officials, oil company staff, or community and youth leaders with benefits to lose. The greatest lesson yet to learn is how to bring these parties to the side of peace and circumvent such obstacles if ending the conflict is not possible.

---

11. See Onigu and Albert, *Community Conflicts.*

7

Nepal: Justice and Security
Nigel Quinney and Colette Rausch

S ince 2006, USIP has developed a distinctive approach to promoting dialogue and cooperation between civil society and security agencies in countries emerging from conflict. The Justice and Security Dialogue (JSD) program has evolved in Nepal, where a ten-year conflict that began in 1996 pitted Maoist insurgents against a repressive monarchy. The fighting killed more than thirteen thousand people and led much of the public to see all security forces as tools of an antidemocratic regime. Eventually, in 2005–2006, a coalition of political parties joined with the Maoists to put an end to monarchical rule and to launch a peace process intended to restore democratic government. But that peace process is fragile and has been buffeted by a surge in crime and constant political turmoil.

JSD seeks to bridge the gulf of mistrust between civilian police and local communities by nurturing communication and cooperation. The program involves a variety of other Nepali actors—the human rights community, the judiciary, other security and justice stakeholders, government at both local and national levels, and the country's political parties, among them—in the process of finding joint solutions to shared problems. What helps set this initiative apart from many other efforts to promote the rule of law in post-conflict countries is its emphasis on process, pragmatism, and partnership. Adherence to these three principles is giving communities the tools, the incentives, and the organizational structure to make JSD locally sustainable and nationally influential.

Broadly defined, the long-term goal of JSD is to help Nepal enhance its public security and usher in a society that respects the rule of law. More specifically and immediately, the goals are to

- educate about the nature and conduct of a society governed by the rule of law;
- build trust by dispelling myths, fostering understanding, and building relationships between civil society and the police at both the local and the national level;
- encourage cooperation in the form of information sharing, joint problem solving, strategy development for strengthening rule of law and security, and constant interaction and discussion;
- deliver concrete results in terms of tackling crimes, respecting human rights, and enhancing security;
- feed local-level ideas into the national policymaking process; and
- develop local capacity and empower local actors so that they gradually assume full control of the dialogue process, ensuring its local relevancy and self-sustainability.

JSD pursues these goals in various ways. At the core of the program are facilitated meetings at which members of the Nepal Police (NP) and civil society formulate, express, and discuss their concerns about the justice and security situation, develop ideas for tackling those challenges, and present those ideas to representatives of political parties and local government administration. Once communication has been established, the program then encourages regular, frequent NP–civil society dialogue at the local level—dialogue that (if all goes well) becomes self-sustaining and generates concrete action to enhance security and respect for human rights and rule of law. The results of local-level dialogue are fed into the policymaking process at the national level either directly through contacts between JSD and senior government officials (who have consistently endorsed JSD) or indirectly via the national-level steering group, made up of top-ranking police officers and nationally respected human rights activists.

This chapter describes and analyzes the evolution of JSD in Nepal since 2006, when the signing of the Comprehensive Peace Agreement ushered in hopes that Nepal would turn from violent conflict to peaceful cooperation within a framework of democracy and the rule of law. During this period, JSD has grown from the fusion of informal partnerships between USIP and

NP officers and human rights activists into a series of nested partnerships between international, national, and local actors. As it has evolved, it has acquired its own momentum, with the national partner orchestrating an array of activities and assembling a large cast of local partners. Local partners have increasingly assumed ownership of JSD and undertaken their own initiatives, and the prospect of JSD becoming fully locally self-sustaining may be just a few years from realization.

The chapter highlights lessons learned, both positive and negative, about the circumstances in which JSD can be effective, the elements of JSD that appear to be vital to its success, and the kinds of missteps and misjudgments that can undercut its effectiveness. USIP has distilled the essence of JSD into a flexible framework that has shaped a pilot program in Sudan and is about to be applied in Iraq and Afghanistan.

First, however, this chapter sketches the background that led to JSD, then outlines the philosophy that underlies it, and compares JSD with other peacebuilding dialogues.

Background

The past twenty years of Nepal's history have been among its most tumultuous—cycles of hope and despair playing out against a revolving backdrop of political accommodation and violent confrontation. Among the many casualties of this turmoil has been the population's faith in the ability and the desire of the security services and the legal system to mete out justice and protect them.

That faith was modest to begin with. More than two hundred years of absolute monarchical rule had left the people of Nepal in no doubt that the police and the judiciary served the king and his courtiers, not any notion of impartial justice. In 1990, however, the first of two "people's movements" was launched by a coalition of leftist and centrist political parties. Faced with a tide of popular discontent, King Birendra was forced to accept constitutional monarchy and to reinstitute multiparty democracy through constitutional reform. But high hopes for a brighter future for one of the region's poorest countries were soon dimmed, with increasing corruption and social and economic inequities continuing to deny most Nepalis access to justice, political power, and economic opportunity.

In 1996, the Communist Party of Nepal—Maoist (CPN-M) declared a "people's war" against the regime. Over the next decade, fighting between the government's security forces and the CPN-M's People's Liberation Army (PLA) claimed more than thirteen thousand lives.[1] Almost all the rural areas of the country fell under the control of the Maoists, who established parallel judicial and governance structures. The insurgents enjoyed the support of many marginalized ethnic groups and castes, as well as backing from the poorest sectors of society. Even those Nepalis who did not agree with the Maoist political agenda and feared the PLA and its often brutal tactics were likely to be equally apprehensive of the security forces, which are alleged to have killed more civilians and committed more human rights abuses than the PLA.[2]

Convinced that multiparty democracy could never defeat the insurgents, in February 2005 King Gyanendra (who had become king after a mysterious massacre of members of the royal family in 2001) declared a state of emergency, suspended civil and political rights, and reinstituted absolute rule. But rather than defeat the Maoists, Gyanendra unwittingly helped them into power. His totalitarian rule drove the seven largest political parties to join forces not only with one another but also with the CPN-M. Together, in late 2005, the eight-party alliance drew up a program aimed at restoring democracy. Just six months later, the second "people's movement" erupted. Nineteen days of violent strikes and mass protests cost twenty-five lives (and widened the divide between the security forces and the public) but succeeded in forcing the king to agree to reinstate the House of Representatives. An interim government was formed and a Comprehensive Peace Agreement between the CPN-M and the government was signed in November 2006.

Hopes grew once again that Nepal would finally achieve a stable, accountable, peaceful political system concerned for the welfare of all Nepalis. The democratic momentum seemed unstoppable—at least for a while. In January 2007, Maoists entered the Interim Parliament, which had stripped the monarchy of its powers and adopted an interim constitution. In April 2007, Maoist leaders became part of the interim government and looked forward to elections in May for a Constituent Assembly that would draft a new constitution. But then the impetus behind the peace process began to stutter. The elections scheduled for May were postponed, first to November

---

1. "A decade-long Maoist insurgency claimed more than 13,000 lives, with the police, the army, and the Maoists all responsible for numerous human rights abuses during the conflict." *Human Rights Watch*, May 22, 2008.

2. For details of human rights abuses by the PLA and the security forces, see International Crisis Group, "Cultures of Impunity," in *Nepal: Peace and Justice*, Asia Report no. 184, January 14, 2010, chapter 3.

and then to April 2008. Meanwhile, outside of parliament, masses of dem-
onstrators were returning to the streets of Kathmandu, and outside of the
capital, a wave of crime and insecurity was washing over the country.

This rising tide of criminality and violence has yet to turn. The border
with India is home to dozens of organized criminal groups engaged in
cross-border smuggling, banditry, killings, extortion, abduction, and human trafficking. In the area north of the border—the lowlands known as
the Terai—ethnic rallies have exploded into violence directed against the
NP, government officials, businesses, and CPN-M groups. Many politicians have been exploiting and exacerbating disaffection among the country's ethnic minorities and poorest citizens, and as a result, more than
thirty armed groups are allied with one or another political party or ethnic
organization.

Nearly every political party has formed its own youth wing, and these
wings behave more like militias than political institutions. Strikes and road
blockades (called *chakkajams*), many of which turn violent, are common. The
capital itself has witnessed numerous *bandhs*—combinations of street protests and general strikes. Each *bandh* can bring the city to a standstill for
days, with tens or hundreds of thousands of young activists camping at in-
tersections and marching through the streets to enforce their party's demand
that nothing (neither shops nor schools nor offices) opens and nothing (neither buses nor cars nor motorcycles) moves.

The political parties in the national government have been reluctant to
take action against youth wings and other quasi-political groups, partly out
of fear of upsetting the country's fragile political raft, partly because they
benefit from it, and partly because the parties themselves like to flex their
political muscle and interfere in policing and the judicial process. Where
once the monarchy put pressure on judges and prosecutors to achieve its
political gains and used the NP to protect its political interests, now numerous supposedly democratic parties vie to do so. Political interference extends
from the highest political levels to the lowest. It also extends from the bustling capital of Kathmandu to the cities of the industrialized lowlands and
the remote villages hidden in the hills and perched on the mountains of
Nepal. Who gets a traffic ticket, who wins a court case, who secures a state
contract: everything is determined by an unholy trinity of political pressure,
physical intimidation, and bribes.

As a culture of lawlessness has grown, so has a culture of impunity. Nepal's
conflict was a very dirty affair, and human rights abuses were all too common.
But, as of January 2010, "there has not been a single prosecution in civilian

courts for any abuses," the International Crisis Group reports. "The cultures of impunity that enabled the crimes in the first place have remained intact, further increasing public distrust and incentives to resort to violence."[3]

A lack of political will to impose the rule of law has been matched by a lack of the capacity to do so. The legal framework is outdated and unclear; criminal and civil law are under the same umbrella, for instance, which creates confusion, and the Police Act and penal laws need updating to adequately address crimes such as kidnapping. In some parts of Nepal, courthouses and legal offices are hard to find, and throughout the country there is a dearth of well-trained, independent prosecutors. Witnesses often refuse to testify in court cases because they fear retribution. Defense lawyers frequently encounter abuse and physical intimidation, even at courthouses.

The NP is particularly hard hit by a lack of resources and operational independence. Unlike the Nepal Army, which has always been a center of political power and has thus enjoyed strong funding, and the Armed Police Force, a well-equipped paramilitary force created in 2001 to combat the insurgency, the NP has few champions in government and suffers from shortfalls in everything from funding to training to equipment. In many remote corners of the country, NP officers are either absent entirely or few and far between, and often unable to speak the language of the local population. Elsewhere, NP posts have to try to combat crime despite severe shortages of logistical equipment such as radios, vehicles, and fuel; despite poor living conditions and low pay; and despite encountering contempt, mistrust, or outright hostility from people who regard the NP as inept, corrupt, or repressive.

This image is not entirely undeserved, not least because standards of recruitment and training have been low, promotion within the organization has traditionally been determined not by merit but by favoritism and nepotism, and political interference is rife. At the same time, however, the NP has been a convenient scapegoat—especially for the government that underfunds it and for the political parties that interfere in its work. It is no surprise that morale within the NP has been very low.

Nor is it surprising that citizens often turn to criminal gangs, rather than the NP, for protection. When victims do try to seek official help, observed one defense lawyer, sometimes they find themselves "victimized by the police, who procrastinate, demand taxi fare to travel to the crime scene, and invite bribes—by the time the police act, the perpetrator is gone."

---

3. International Crisis Group, *Nepal: Peace and Justice*, executive summary.

Standards of crime scene investigation vary wildly, from excellent to abysmal. When a police officer is transferred from one district to another, the cases that he or she has been handling often fizzle out. Some innocent people detained by the police complain that they are beaten while in custody. And there are so few public defenders that the police typically interrogate suspects and witnesses with no attorney present. "The phrase *rule of law*," said another defense lawyer, "makes a mockery of lawlessness in our country—it's gone that far."[4]

Three Underlying Principles

The JSD program has developed in the field, evolving in response to Nepal's emerging needs and to a growing recognition—by domestic and foreign actors—of how those needs might be addressed. Changes in the political and security environment have presented both challenges and opportunities. Some of those challenges have been surmounted; others have called for plans and schedules to be rewritten or even abandoned. Where opportunities have been taken, they have occasionally led to dead ends, but more often they have led to further avenues for productive work.

But though JSD has not grown according to a predetermined strategy or blueprint, it has from its early days adhered to three general principles that together form its basic methodology. Those principles are the three P's of partnership, process, and pragmatism. Individually, each element can have a significant impact on the content and conduct of dialogue, but collectively, that impact is multiplied many times over.

JSD depends on forming a variety of partnerships at different levels: international-national, national-local, NP–civil society, and so forth. These partnerships are crucial for three reasons. First, JSD does not insist on particular diagnoses or impose particular prescriptions. To the contrary, JSD assumes that the actors at a given level are best equipped to understand and address problems at that level. Second, action at one level will generate sustainable results only if supported at other levels. Third, partnerships enable the most efficient division of labor; instead of one actor providing everything, each actor contributes the resources (intellectual, financial, operational, human, political, and so on) that actor is best equipped to provide. The ties between partners are sustained and strengthened by constant consultation and by col-

---

4. These views were expressed during a meeting between JSD representatives and women attorneys in the Hotel Himalaya in Kathmandu, Friday, April 30, 2010. A record of the discussion is in the authors' files.

laboration in the conceptualization as well as the implementation of programs. The partners treat each other as partners, not as donors or recipients, nor as clients or competitors.

The process of working together is seen as no less important than the accomplishment of specific goals. By emphasizing process, JSD gives stakeholders the opportunity to set their own objectives and the tools with which to pursue them sustainably. This approach is highly appropriate for a program that seeks to promote the rule of law, because a secure and just society is one that allows all its members to express their concerns, enables them to work with others to address those concerns, and encourages them to see that justice and security are two sides of the same coin. By engaging in a process like the JSD—which is not a negotiation but an attempt to create synergy— a society moves closer toward a society that respects the rule of law.

In JSD, the aim is not merely to open lines of communication between mistrustful groups but also to create a sense of accomplishment among participants and to make a pragmatic difference in people's lives. Processes such as fostering mutual understanding, sharing information, and joint problem solving are intended to lead to concrete improvements in the levels of justice and security within the society. JSD teaches stakeholders techniques and exposes them to ideas that they can take and apply in the field, making a tangible difference to their own lives rather than generating results solely to satisfy criteria established by international donors (see the appendix for a summary of how these principles have been implemented as JSD has evolved).

None of these three elements is unique to JSD, of course. All forms of facilitated dialogue value inclusivity, respectfulness, transparency, openness, and authenticity. All emphasize the process of learning how to stop lecturing the other side and start listening to it. Like JSD, they seek to enhance mutual understanding, build trust, and discover shared interest, and "reframe the conflict from a zero-sum, mutual-blame situation, to a more nuanced understanding of mutual needs."[5]

Some dialogues do not try to move beyond this step. They leave it to their participants to decide if and how to build on what they have learned in the dialogue. The Dartmouth Conference, for example, brought together influential figures outside (temporarily, at least) of government over the course of several decades to build trust and understanding between the elites of the

---

5. Heidi and Guy Burgess, *Understanding Track II Diplomacy: Peacemaker's Toolkit* (Washington, DC: U.S. Institute of Peace, 2010). The authors are also grateful to Maria Jessop and Anthony Wanis-St. John for their observations on facilitated dialogue in general and on JSD in particular.

Soviet Union and United States.[6] Participants were expected to discuss what they had heard and learned with members of their governments, but there was usually no explicit Dartmouth mechanism for translating enhanced understanding into action. JSD, by contrast, has created a process that offers numerous ways to make this transition. For instance, as this chapter describes, JSD takes ideas voiced at the local level and feeds them directly into the national policymaking process.

In terms of pragmatic goals, many dialogues try to help their participants use their newly acquired mutual understanding to engage in joint problem-solving, analyzing the nature of their conflict and, perhaps, charting a course to move beyond it. Numerous examples of facilitated dialogues, and some of ventures in the field of interactive conflict resolution, have encouraged participants to brainstorm and thrash out the terms of a peace agreement. The Inter-Tajik Dialogue, for instance, brought together influential but nongovernmental figures to break down mistrust and foster discussion of how to resolve Tajikistan's civil war.[7] Other Track II efforts have even more concrete goals. For instance, a problem-solving workshop was held in May 1996 in Bosnia-Herzegovina between Catholic and Muslim religious people to discuss how they might support the creation of a new water system that would serve both a predominantly Christian city and a mainly Muslim one.[8] Concrete (sometimes literally) results are also pursued by peace education projects that bring together members of opposing sides to construct organizations, institutions, and even buildings that will symbolize or promote reconciliation.

In JSD dialogues, the progression from improved understanding to cooperating on joint proposals is built into the dialogue itself. And participants are encouraged not only to turn joint proposals into joint action subsequent to a dialogue session but also to develop an ever-expanding variety of joint activities. One of the most distinctive aspects of JSD is that its structure enables cooperative relationships to be built on multiple levels simultaneously: geographically, at the local and the national levels; professionally, at junior as well as senior levels; socially, at the grassroots, among the middle strata of society, and within the elite.

---

6. For more information, see James Voorhees, *Dialogue Sustained: The Multilevel Peace Process and the Dartmouth Conference* (Washington, DC: U.S. Institute of Peace, 2002).

7. Harold Saunders, "Prenegotiation and Circum-negotiation: Arenas of the Peace Process," in *Managing Global Chaos*, edited by Chester Crocker, Fen Hampson, and Pamela Aall (Washington, DC: U.S. Institute of Peace, 1996), 419–432.

8. See David Steele, "Peacebuilding in the Former Yugoslavia," in *Interfaith Dialogue and Peacebuilding*, edited by David R. Smock (Washington, DC: U.S. Institute of Peace, 2002), 85.

JSD's emphasis on partnership is akin to the efforts by other dialogues to create a sense of "joint ownership." The closeness and the openness of the partnerships that characterize JSD are unusual, however. Also distinctive is JSD's progression from a partnership initiated by international and national-level actors—but highly responsive to local-level concerns and highly committed to empowering local actors—to a partnership in which local stakeholders decide for themselves the content and structure of their dialogue while the national and international partners take a back seat and offer support only when requested. In Nepal, JSD's multitiered partnerships allow the program to operate at different levels of society—grassroots, mid-level, and elite—and to serve as a conduit between them.

A Fusion of Partnerships

JSD has evolved organically, as a response to perceived needs and to the discovery of resources (chiefly, human resources) available to address that need. JSD was not an attempt to implement a particular theory or type of facilitated dialogue. To be sure, its creators were informed by their knowledge of and experience with a wide variety of Track 2 activities, from training to dialogues, public education to interactive conflict resolution. They were also informed by their experiences with working with security forces, or in some cases, being witness to abuses by the security forces. But the creators felt their way forward, rather than following a script or map. Where they encountered resistance or indifference, they typically pulled back and reassessed their options; where they found receptive stakeholders and inventive ideas, they moved ahead.

Although tied to no theory or preconceived strategy, JSD's founders were wedded to a broad philosophy that guided JSD's formation and that continues to shape its activities. The most basic tenet of that philosophy is that no one person or organization has all the answers to promoting dialogue and the rule of law in societies emerging from conflict. Outsiders may have technical expertise but not local knowledge; insiders may understand the dynamics of local conflicts but not how to escape them. The immediate solution, therefore, is to bring all parties together and pool their talents and resources in a common endeavor to nurture communication, education, and cooperation. The long-term solution is to empower local actors with the technical knowledge, hands-on experience, and confidence that will enable them to gradually assume full control of the dialogue process.

Partnerships offer the most effective model for this joint endeavor because, unlike donor-recipient or client-vendor relationships, they have no vertical hierarchies and encourage the two-way transmission of ideas. As it has turned out, JSD has developed a cascading set of partnerships: an international partner in the shape of the Rule of Law program at USIP's Washington office; a national partner composed of USIP's representatives in Kathmandu and a high-level focal group made up of high-ranking NP officers and leading Nepali human rights advocates; and numerous local partnerships with a wide range of Nepalese stakeholders, including local-level NGOs. This elaborate system of partnerships was not in anyone's mind, however, when a team from USIP's Rule of Law Program first visited Nepal.

In the spring of 2006, Colette Rausch, then deputy director of the Rule of Law program, and Vivienne O'Connor, then project officer for rule of law at the Irish Center for Human Rights, traveled to Nepal to consult with local actors and conduct a case study for a project titled "Model Codes for Post-Conflict Criminal Justice." They were en route to Kathmandu when Nepal's second people's movement erupted, prompting them to change the focus of their visit. They arrived in Nepal on the day its king was deposed. Not only had most U.S. officials left Nepal due to the violence, but many other foreign organizations had done the same, leaving the USIP team with a unique opportunity to help wherever needed.

Rausch, having lived and worked in post-conflict countries such as Afghanistan, Bosnia, and Kosovo, envisioned a number of rule of law challenges that Nepal would face. She and O'Connor began meeting with representatives of a very wide range of parties, groups, and viewpoints to discover how best USIP could be of assistance. They consulted with civil society on transitional justice options and organized workshops on the subject, put together CDs of resources on constitution making, and distributed books on transitional justice to Nepal's civil society and government representatives. They knew from experience with other transitional states that Nepal was about to be descended upon by a great many well-meaning but not necessarily helpful foreign donors and organizations, each with its own agenda. They thought it critical to ask Nepalis, "What do *you* think? Speak up, empower yourself, so you're on an equal footing with the donors and others who are coming." They also foretold of the not-so-savory players likely to capitalize on the power vacuum and insecurity created by the king's sudden departure. These players would include criminal gangs, violent splinter groups, and political spoilers.

Thanks to colleagues who had contacts within the NP, Rausch and O'Connor began meeting with several high-level NP officials, who provided unvarnished facts about the country's rule of law situation. When Rausch returned to the United States, she arranged with her former office at the U.S. Department of Justice for three senior NP officers (Surendra Shah, Bigyan Sharma, and Upendra Aryal) to come to Washington in October 2006 to learn about serious crimes challenges, strategic planning, and rule of law in transition from conflict to democratic governance.

USIP had already been working on rule of law initiatives in transitional states in general, and, while in Washington, the NP officers expressed interest in a variety of USIP projects, including the model codes for post-conflict criminal justice and the recently published volume *Combating Serious Crimes in Postconflict Societies*, which offered guidance on tackling organized and other destabilizing crimes in societies emerging from conflict.[9] Rausch provided copies to the NP, whose leadership was looking for assistance that might help it manage its own transition from a security service widely seen as corrupt, incompetent, and a tool of a repressive government into a professional, independent police force accountable to the public as a whole. *Combating Serious Crimes* was subsequently translated into Nepali and thousands of copies were distributed to government officials, NP officers, lawyers, prosecutors, and members of civil society throughout the country. As of late 2010, the Nepali edition was about to be reprinted for a third time. The NP and the Attorney General's Office have also requested that USIP's *Model Codes for Post-Conflict Criminal Justice* be translated into Nepali and widely distributed.[10]

Among the many foreign agencies and NGOs establishing a presence in Nepal as the country edged toward an end of its internal conflict, USIP had certain advantages in the eyes of the NP. It could offer practical help and pertinent expertise as well as encouragement. It did not condemn the entire NP as corrupt and undemocratic in its policing, as some other organizations had done. It had high-level contacts within the U.S. government, which the NP suspected might be of assistance to the NP in enlisting support within its own government for transforming the NP into a publicly accountable force. USIP was not linked with any political group or agenda within Nepal.

9.   Colette Rausch, ed., *Combating Serious Crimes in Postconflict Societies: A Handbook for Policymakers and Practitioners* (Washington, DC: U.S. Institute of Peace, 2006).

10. As of 2010, two volumes of model codes have been published: *Model Codes for Post-Conflict Criminal Justice*, edited by Colette Rausch and Vivienne O'Connor, vol. 1, *Model Criminal Code*, and vol. 2, *Model Code of Criminal Procedure* (Washington, DC: U.S. Institute of Peace Press, 2007–8). A third volume containing a Model Detention Act is forthcoming.

And USIP was voicing, and seemed to be demonstrating, a commitment to helping the NP deal with the challenges to security and justice posed by a society emerging from conflict.

The appetite among NP's leaders for reform and their apparent readiness to accept help encouraged Rausch to seek to develop the relationship. She saw the opportunity for USIP to move beyond providing useful resources and to start working *jointly* with the NP. Exactly how such an endeavor might manifest itself was not yet clear, but Rausch, like the NP, was receptive to the notion of forming a long-term partnership, an arrangement in which both partners would contribute ideas and resources in pursuit of the shared goal of combating destabilizing crime and promoting security within the country.

At the same time, Rausch also continued developing a relationship with Nepal's civil society. Her long-term aim, as with the NP, was to find people who would work on an equal footing with USIP—people who would not just attend a workshop or implement a program but also help to conceive and design it. Several of the qualities that had cemented USIP's standing with the NP—the ability to offer practical help, pertinent expertise, high-level contacts, political independence, and commitment—were also high on Rausch's list of criteria for a civil society partner. She also wanted to find a partner who was committed to promoting peace and justice rather than to advancing their own personal agendas.

With these criteria in mind, USIP enlisted the help of Shobhakar Budhathoki, a nationally known human rights defender and conflict resolution practitioner based in Nepal, and Karon Cochran-Budhathoki, a conflict resolution specialist also based in Nepal. The first thing they were asked to do was to coordinate a workshop on security-sector reform in Kathmandu in late August 2006, as the negotiations that would yield the CPA approached their conclusion. The workshop gave the pair an opportunity to demonstrate not only their grasp of security and rule of law issues but also their organizational abilities and their contacts and credibility with members of Nepal's civil society.

After working with her NP partners and her civil society partners separately, Rausch broached the idea of the two meeting to explore common ground and—perhaps—create the foundations for a larger dialogue. The three senior NP officers who were then visiting Washington, D.C., responded enthusiastically to the idea. The officers were well aware that the NP needed help in rebuilding relations with civil society, which had never been good historically and had taken a severe battering during the civil war, when the NP were deployed on the front lines of the fight against the Maoist insurgents. Many members of the NP were highly reluctant to countenance civilian "interference" in police business and especially in the sensitive matter of reform of the NP, but these three high-ranking officers saw the advantages of getting civilian input. "When the idea of working with Shobhakar and Karon in JSD arose," recalled one of those officers, Surendra Shah, then a senior superintendent and now a deputy inspector general in the NP, "we realized we can do it and we have to do it. It's very important for civil society to work with us, and whether they will do so depends on how they perceive us. If we, the police, don't face up to our weaknesses, we'll never move ahead."[11]

The Budhathokis were initially circumspect, their years of monitoring human rights abuses before and during the people's war having left them wary of Nepal's security services, but agreed to meet with the three officers and establish lines of communication. The first meeting was a rather formal encounter, but less frosty than might have been expected, and all agreed to meet again. Over the next few months, a sense of trust developed and personal relationships grew, nurtured by cooperation on specific issues (such as investigating allegations of human rights abuses) and by a common goal: to see the NP become a professional, accountable institution and Nepal become a state governed by the rule of law.

In early 2007, the Budhathokis became the formal national partner to USIP's international partner. Karon became official USIP representative in Nepal and her husband Shobhakar became USIP national adviser. In a country with formidable logistical challenges—such as regular power outages for up to sixteen hours a day, monsoon floods that can cut off part of the country, and political unrest that can make travel even within the capital city difficult or dangerous—they set about establishing an office in Kathmandu that could design, orchestrate, and implement projects both large and small. As they were to discover, such challenges were not usually insurmountable, but they certainly could disrupt plans and schedules.

The NP leaders assumed a more informal role, but were to be a key component of the national partnership, advocating for JSD's goals within government circles, putting JSD's principles into practice in the daily work of the NP, and helping devise JSD strategy and monitor its implementation by participating in a national focal group.

Two prominent human rights activists—Kapil Shrestha and Sushil Pyakurel—accepted invitations to become part of the focal group. As

---

11. Interview by author with Surendra Shah, Kathmandu, April 30, 2010. All other quotations from Surendra Shah are taken from this interview.

Pyakurel, a leading figure within Nepal's human rights community for more than twenty years, noted, the timing was excellent. This was not the first time Nepalis had contemplated reforming the country's justice and security institutions. In the immediate aftermath of the first people's movements, some human rights activists had discussed security-sector reform, and since then the government had periodically formed commissions to study the subject. Nothing concrete had ever resulted, however—in part because the push for reform had come not from the police or the people but from above, and in part because there had been no broader peace process to inspire hope that significant change was really possible and sustainable. "Then Shobhakar brought in this idea and asked me to become involved," Pyakurel recalled. "The beauty of the idea is that all stakeholders are involved from the start."[12]

The partnership between senior NP officers and human rights defenders embodies a central tenet of JSD, that justice and security are indivisible. Justice is understood to mean not only an independent judiciary and due process of law but also popular conceptions of fairness, equality of treatment, and accountability. Security is interpreted broadly to mean a society that not only maintains civil order and enforces laws but also respects human rights and reflects social diversity; indeed, these components of security are seen as mutually supportive and security as indivisible. In the words of Surendra Shah, "The problem is security. And that's not my problem or civil society's problem—it's everyone's problem."

An Experiment in the Capital

Together, the partners began to design a program of facilitated dialogue and to solicit interest from potential participants: high-ranking figures in the security forces, senior government officials (national and regional), political leaders, and eminent figures in civil society and the NGO community. The aim was to create and cultivate a series of interconnected personal relationships. Nepal's culture puts a high premium on personal ties, and it is difficult to get anything done without first building a reservoir of hospitality, understanding, and trust over coffee or dinner.

The first public event was a four-day discussion in Kathmandu in February 2007, a month that witnessed Maoist rallies in the capital and rising violence across the Terai as Madhesi groups pressed for greater political

12. Interview by author with Sushil Pyakurel, Kathmandu, April 29, 2010. All quotations from Sushil are taken from this interview.

representation. Evidence of the fragility and uneven progress of the peace process was everywhere. For example, more than fifty police posts in the east only recently reestablished had to be closed again because of the growing level of violence.[13]

The dialogue in Kathmandu was facilitated by Rausch, O'Connor, and former OSCE senior police adviser Richard Monk, who offered ideas on rule of law principles and shared their experiences with Nepali participants, who in turn discussed how the concepts of justice and security fit within the country's context. The first day, civil society representatives from legal groups, development organizations, media, human rights groups, and lower caste and marginalized ethnic groups discussed their concerns about Nepal's security situation and proposed steps to enhance the provision of justice. The second day, mid- and high-ranking NP officers discussed the same issues. The third day, civil society and the NP developed a joint list of high-priority issues. And on the fourth day, this list was presented to political party representatives, who then offered their comments and suggestions. This sequence of meetings would form the model for subsequent JSD dialogues.

Taking JSD to the Districts

The positive response from participants in the Kathmandu experiments persuaded the JSD partners to widen both the reach and the scope of the dialogues—from beyond the capital into the Terai, and to include lower-ranking officials and officers.

Whereas Rausch, O'Connor, and Monk had facilitated the dialogue in Kathmandu in February, with the Budhathokis' support, for the district sessions the Budhathokis not only organized the dialogues but also ran them. The national partner had developed the capacity to do so, and a constant in-country presence was critical to building the relationships with Nepali stakeholders on which the dialogues would depend.

The Budhathokis established contact with a large number of actors throughout the Terai. Stakeholder input was considered critical. "When we approached local communities, we didn't just tell them about the program," Karon explains. "Our first step was actually to go in and talk to them about what they wanted and what they felt they needed—and then work with them to hone an approach that fit their needs while advancing the broad

---

13. See "OCHA Nepal Situation Overview," no. 10, February 17, 2007, http://www.internal-displace ment.org/8025708F004CE90B/(httpDocuments)/CB1775A9C65937C1C125728A003D062F/ $file/2007-2-22-OCHA-Situation-Overview-feb.pdf.

goals of the project." This step came at a cost. For JSD to be sustainable, breadth and depth of stakeholder involvement are crucial, but the price is a slower process.

The dialogues were to be held in the districts facing the most severe security problems: refugee camps and cantonment sites, high levels of poverty and crime, and active ethnic- or regional-based movements. In such districts, violence or the threat of violence was never far away.

In preparing for the district dialogues, the international and national partners decided to extend the concept of partnership to the local level. A key step in this process was to partner with the Informal Sector Service Center (INSEC), a Nepali human rights NGO founded by Sushil Pyakurel. Headquartered in Kathmandu, INSEC has five regional offices and more than forty local networks. INSEC thus gave JSD instant access to an organizational network that spanned almost the entire country.

Finding suitable local partners was not always straightforward. Nepal has a legacy of nepotism and favoritism that colors many institutions and organizations. JSD could not afford to be seen as partnering with NGOs with a reputation for nepotism or corruption. USIP's zero tolerance in this respect initially provoked some dissatisfaction. The geographic spread of local partners also made oversight of their activities more difficult. A regional oversight mechanism that placed additional demands on INSEC was put in place, as were strict financial reporting and oversight mechanisms. Unprofessionalism and corruption led to the dissolution of one partner relationship in one district.

The net effect of insisting on impartiality, however, was positive. It helped USIP acquire a reputation as impartial and trustworthy, and it meant that both USIP and local communities could have faith in the fairness and professionalism of the local partners. In all, the Budhathokis developed partnerships with twenty organizations, including INSEC and other NGOs. Those local partners entrusted with facilitating dialogues received two or more days of training in how to communicate the goals of JSD, articulate rule of law principles in locally relevant terms, and encourage candid discussion and focus debate on key subject areas.

Between May and August 2007, a series of six dialogues, each lasting at least two days, were conducted in different districts of the Terai.[14] No fewer than 125 police personnel, 144 civil society members, and 56 government and political party representatives participated. Some attended because their

14. This description of the format and conduct of these dialogues draws on a series of internal reports prepared by Shobhakar Budhathoki and Karon Cochran-Budhathoki.

superiors in Kathmandu had pressured them to do so—demonstrating the importance of JSD first building support at the national level. Most, however, came because they were eager to take advantage of this rare opportunity to discuss security and rule of law issues with groups with whom they usually had little communication.

The participants were numerous and diverse. Individuals varied in terms of rank (junior NP constables to deputy inspector generals), profession (lawyers were joined by journalists, teachers, business people, and writers), area of interest (participating NGOs championed, for instance, human rights, women's rights, development, and indigenous peoples), and political affiliation (ten political parties were represented). Efforts were also made to ensure significant participation by women and ethnic groups. The same concern for diversity is reflected in the staff at the national partner's offices in Kathmandu.

The format of these provincial dialogues was similar to that of the dialogue held in February in the capital. On the first day, the facilitators introduced general principles and then each side met on its own to discuss its concerns.

For the NP, typical concerns ranged from problems within the NP such as poor pay and inadequate equipment to the effects of political disunity at the national level and political interference at the local level. Civil society participants identified issues such as the NP's unwillingness or inability to investigate rape cases, political interference in arresting or punishing culprits, victims' lack of access to the courts, and the tendency of the state and the NP to ignore or at least undervalue civil society.

On the second day, each side presented its thoughts and ideas and jointly devised possible solutions. Initially, this encounter could be frosty, accusatory, or highly guarded, but in most cases the two sides found themselves surprised by the extent of their agreement.

The joint recommendations were typically numerous and varied. Some recommendations focused on day-to-day policing, such as calls for NP officers to be better trained, equipped, housed, and paid, and for social crimes such as polygamy and prostitution to be addressed through community policing programs. Many other suggestions, however, roamed across subjects such as the responsibilities of civil society, gaps in the legal framework, judicial corruption, obstacles to the peace process, the need for education, respect for women's rights, the status of minorities, and politics. In one form or another, politics figured prominently. The NP and civil society discovered that they both wanted to see a prompt end to political interference in policing and prosecuting cases, tighter control by political parties of their youth wings, fewer and better disciplined *bandhs*, the political will to tackle the culture of impunity, and politicians and government officials to stop viewing the NP as a tool of the state and to start seeing it as a service to the public.

Perhaps because politics was in the cross-hairs of many complaints, the politicians tended to react uncomfortably or defensively. For the most part, however, the party representatives did publicly affirm the need to end corruption, impunity, and political interference. They also endorsed in general terms the recommendations they heard—although they rarely declared that they would themselves plan and push for implementation of a specific proposal.

Many party representatives were guarded in their contributions to the dialogues, but most other participants spoke candidly, if not at the outset of the dialogues then soon thereafter. Several factors help explain this openness. One is the degree of commitment to the dialogues shown by high-ranking local government officials responsible for local security and by senior NP officers. The latter not only attended but also displayed a willingness to be open and self-critical, which encouraged lower-ranking officers to follow suit. Equally important was the facilitators' ability to create an open, nonjudgmental atmosphere, to explain the win-win nature of reform of the justice and security sectors, and to guide discussion from expressions of grievance to formulations of possible solutions.

A New Experience and Understanding

Written and oral feedback revealed that this was the first time many of the participants had sat down in a discussion with both the NP and civil society to talk openly and constructively about the local security situation. Participants were particularly excited that their opinions and ideas would be relayed to the central policymaking level, which, many felt, is where reform of the security and justice system should begin.

Both police and civil society participants said they had gained a better understanding of the roles they should play in a transitioning society and the importance of working together. Many NP officials said that the dialogues allowed them to see themselves, for the first time, as human rights defenders and public servants—roles they were proud to have. Even veterans of the human rights movement found that their perceptions of the NP had changed. Sushil Pyakurel notes that his generation had come to see the police purely as a tool of repression. Human rights activists had always "talked about human rights but not about who will protect human rights. But now, when you talk about human rights, about impunity, one needs to contemplate working with the police. If cases are not handled properly, you will not get justice. [JSD] has broadened our vision."

The dialogues provided an opportunity to begin building consensus in civil society and understand the need for it. Dialogues tended to be noticeably more constructive in districts and regions where civil society organizations and individuals are accustomed to working together and correspondingly less constructive where there is more donor activity and less coordination.

The tenor and content of each conversation were also affected by the level of violence and insecurity within each district. In those areas facing daily and widespread violence from armed groups, security challenges were more easily identified, and no one questioned the need for the NP and civil society to work together.[15]

Deepening and Broadening JSD

The success of the district dialogues, like that of those in Kathmandu, presented a question for the JSD partners: what next?

One obvious answer was to maintain and develop the momentum already achieved in the districts where the dialogues had been held. A great deal can often be accomplished with only modest funds—a monthly local meeting, for instance, can be arranged and refreshments supplied for as little $20. Moreover, regular interaction allows participants to act on some of the concerns identified at the dialogue, underlining its practical value. Two examples from the district of Kailali illustrate the ways in which the dialogue has prompted subsequent action to mitigate local conflict and strengthen the rule of law. In one case, an NP senior officer, with support from civil society that had grown from the dialogue, asked local CPM-N leaders for help in recovering NP vehicles that had been taken by Maoist cadres. The next day all the vehicles were returned. In another instance, the NP found itself unable to resolve a violent land dispute in which members of an indigenous group were burning huts belonging to local laborers. The police asked for the help of the individual who had been selected during the JSD sessions as the civil society contact person. That person promptly arrived on the scene and, working with the NP, was able to prevent any further homes being torched.

---

15. Much of these two paragraphs is taken from an internal report by USIP's representatives in Kathmandu, dated September 5, 2007, on the dialogues in Dhangadhi, Bhadrapur, Bharatapur, and Butwal.

Efforts to build on the original dialogues were also needed to try to counter the discouragement experienced in districts where JSD participants had discovered that attempts to undermine the principles of the rule of law continued much as before. In such areas, constant interaction with stakeholders would be vital to maintain enthusiasm. The necessary investment of time and energy would reinforce the impression that the JSD program was a long-term initiative, and thus different from many other donor-funded NGO activities launched in Nepal.

Another question was whether the results of the dialogues suggested the need to develop entirely new programming. The first step in this direction was to review and distill the findings of the dialogues in a report released with some fanfare at Kathmandu's Hotel Himalaya in September 2007. A large room at the hotel was packed with well-known figures from Nepal's civil society and the NP, and included several prominent international figures, such as Lord Alderdice, who talked about his experience in the Northern Ireland peace process. The centerpiece of the discussion was the report, *Nepal in Transition: Strengthening Security and the Rule of Law*, which was organized around six categories of recommendations: law and order, politics and security, legal reform and the judiciary, civil society, and the NP.[16]

The response to the report was encouraging, the Home Ministry (the government department responsible for the security services) and the human rights and legal rights communities expressing interest in JSD's early results. NP leadership felt that its decision to support the dialogues from the start had been vindicated. However small the percentage of the NP participating in the initial dialogues, and despite some resistance within the organization, NP's leadership was impressed, and accepted that in the NP, as in any established institution, cultural change needs to be nurtured very patiently.

In December, the national and international partners invited the focal group—three NP officers and one human rights defender—to Washington, D.C., to discuss additional programming on security and the rule of law. Throughout the discussion, the partners were careful not to impose their own ideas and instead sought to tease out and then help develop suggestions from the focal group members.

The session and follow-up discussions produced a four-part program with clear, pragmatic goals:

---

16. Colette Rausch, Shobhakar Budhathoki, and Karon Cochran-Budhathoki, *Nepal in Transition: Strengthening Security and the Rule of Law* (Washington, DC: U.S. Institute of Peace, September 2007).

- development of an NP–civil society forum to enable frequent police-community interaction;
- community engagement on issues identified in the survey to develop trust and communication between the NP and the public;
- a baseline survey of attitudes toward security and access to justice, the results of which would provide a unique resource on which to develop more effective strategies; and
- interactive programs between the police and prosecutors' offices to improve mutual understanding and professional cooperation.

Within a year, the international partner obtained funding for this two-year project from the U.S. State Department's International Narcotics and Law Enforcement Bureau (INL).

Concrete Gains

The first element in the program quickly yielded results. In the spring of 2009, adopting the name the Security and Rule of Law Dialogue Center (SRLDC), the police–civil society forum acquired an office, meeting space, and resource center in the eastern Terai city of Britnagar. The national partner and other members of the focal group met with local government officials, NP officers in charge of the region and district, members of civil society, political parties, and ethnic and other marginalized groups to discuss the center and its objectives, and to cultivate support for dialogue.

By the end of 2009, four roundtable dialogues had been held. The first focused on the security situation in the surrounding district of Morang. Another examined the challenges faced by the culturally distinct Madhesi community—which has long considered itself discriminated against by the Nepal state. After the dialogue, the SRLDC was also asked to mediate between a group of Madhesi youth and a local NGO (which was receiving funds from USAID) about the NGO's hiring practices. SRLDC persuaded the two sides to discuss their concerns and positions, and together they hammered out an agreement.

Two other dialogues examined why youth seem to increasingly participate in lawless and violent activities and what young people themselves could do to reverse that trend. Representatives from the youth and student wings of political parties, members of civil society organizations working on youth issues, local government officials, and senior NP officers pinpointed as problems the general sense of hopelessness among youth, mobilization of youth groups as vigilantes by political parties, and increased drug and cross-border crimes. Participants—numbering almost one hundred—at the second dialogue agreed on the nine-point Birat Youth Declaration and promised to work together with the NP and civil society to strengthen security and the rule of law. A steering committee, a secretariat, and an advisory committee were subsequently formed to mobilize youths and students for constructive activities. The impact has been dramatic. According to the NP, in the district of Morang "violent demonstrations carried out by youths decreased more than 80 percent because of their involvement in the USIP program that established lines of communication and cooperation between the police and youth, and allowed the police to engage the youth in constructive activities."[17]

In 2010 and 2011, the scope of the dialogues expanded further to encompass areas such as interfaith interaction and women's rights.

Surveying Public Opinion

Another part of the program was even more ambitious, namely, a survey of public and professional attitudes toward access to security and justice in Nepal. The fundamental goal was to establish a baseline of opinion to inform and inspire government and NP efforts to reform the security and justice systems, and that could be used again in the future. Between August and October 2009, 100 specially trained surveyors conducted nearly 13,000 surveys in 120 villages and towns throughout Nepal. In some cases, they had to walk for four or five days through torrential rain and over difficult terrain to reach their assigned district. Everywhere they went, they found the NP supportive and political leaders cooperative, thanks to the extensive consultation with stakeholders that the Budhathokis had conducted before and during the survey, and thanks also to the support of national political and NP leaders for the effort. More than a hundred interviews were also conducted with high-ranking officials, leaders of civil society, prominent members of the judiciary and legal profession, and political party leaders. Fifteen focus group discussions were also held

The results were analyzed by a team of data specialists and published in early 2011. The report reveals a public worried by multiple challenges to the rule of law, skeptical of the NP's capacity or willingness to investigate crime, suspicious of corruption in the police and the judiciary, prepared to seek redress for perceived injustices outside the legal system, and highly critical of the role of political parties in all sorts of crime. It also indicates that the

---

17. Letter from the Metropolitan Police Commissioner's Office in Kathmandu to USIP, February 21, 2011.

public has not abandoned hope that the system can be made to work, and it sees a central role in that system for the NP.[18]

Toward a Sustainable Future?

The results in Nepal persuaded INL to extend funding for the program eighteen months, through 2012. Programming will focus on three areas:

- introducing the concept of the SRLDC to between eight and ten additional districts, helping local partners and local stakeholders establish and assume ownership of the process of regular dialogue;
- developing the capacity of the NP and of partner organizations through a series of workshops on community-oriented policing and the administration of rule of law programs; and
- evaluating the impact of dialogue and community engagement.

The ambition of this program is to strengthen security and the rule of law at the district and community levels by strengthening links between all stakeholders, by enhancing community policing skills and awareness, and by enabling JSD's local partners to assume full ownership of the process of dialogue and cooperation—that is, to make JSD sustainable.

The continuing need for the program is not in question. Since the signing of the CPA in 2006, the peace process has made some progress, but it tends to stumble forward—and sometimes to totter backward. Its progress is intermittent, uncertain, and marked by successive crises and incessant bickering among the major parties. Two key steps to the country's future—integrating Maoist combatants into the state's security forces and drafting a new constitution—have been obstructed with no less energy than they have been debated. Disunity in Kathmandu is matched by disorder in the provinces, where armed political and ethnic groups engage in a mixture of disruptive and often violent protest and crime, both organized and disorganized.

In such an environment, JSD is invaluable in generating the cooperation and consensus that can act as a counterweight to conflict and disunity. JSD is a way of demonstrating to all Nepalis that they have similar hopes and fears and that they can best realize their hopes and cast aside those fears by working together.

---

18. For a detailed description of the survey results, see Karon-Cochran Budhathoki, *Calling for Security and Justice in Nepal: Citizens' Perspectives on the Rule of Law and the Role of the Nepal Police* (Washington, DC: U.S. Institute of Peace, 2011).

But if JSD is to make a real difference, it needs to endure. And if it is to endure, it must be locally sustainable. Thus implementation of the three-part JSD program over next two years will be critical. Whether JSD will have rooted itself deeply into Nepali soil by the end of that time is uncertain. The signs are promising, however. "It will take a long time to achieve sustainability," Sushil observed, "but something has started to happen. Already, the process of interaction has started. All the stakeholders are already involved. How the government responds to publication of the survey results will be very important. Expectations have been raised and must be fulfilled. The government must own the findings of the report and implement them. It will take time. But all the ingredients are there."

Lessons Learned

Five years of work in Nepal has taught the JSD partners several important lessons, both positive and negative, about the conditions, expectations, and approaches that can facilitate or frustrate the effectiveness of the dialogue.

• *Don't launch JSD until the time is right.*
The experience in Nepal suggests that JSD must await its own kind of ripe moment. This comes when two separate but related conditions are present. First, security forces (or some part of them) recognize that they cannot do their job without greater community support and are willing to recognize their own shortcomings and invite discussion on how to improve them. Second, the community's reluctance to cooperate with the security forces—inspired by mistrust and fear of the security forces or fear of being punished by criminals or insurgents for collaboration—is overtaken by the community's readiness to cooperate—inspired by growing desperation with rising crime and violence or by growing optimism that a more secure and just society is attainable.

The security forces and the community will not always embark on a path of dialogue and cooperation, however, unless an external actor encourages them to see that such a path exists, persuades them that the other side is willing to take it, and helps them take the first steps.

• *Be patient and flexible.*
The international partner must be committed to the program yet give the national partner the space and the time to make real progress and to adapt to evolving circumstances. Donors often grow frustrated because their plans are

reworked early and often when put into practice in the field, and impatient because funded projects seem to be yielding only modest results, if any. "But then you discover," Rausch remarked, "how it takes only one person or a few people to start something. You don't need everyone on board at the start. One person with a vision can plant a seed that will grow into something astounding. But the seed needs time to grow."

Many donors are impatient and demand a stream of reports chronicling constant achievement, even when nothing has been achieved. "Unlike some other organizations," Cochran-Budhathoki explained, "USIP does not value reporting for the sake of the report itself but for what it says about the genuine impact [of the program] on the ground in the lives of the people, which you can't always measure very well. It's not about how many people showed up at the meeting but about what they discussed and whether they've been talking to each other since then. It's not about how many books have been distributed but about who has read them and how they have used the information in them. USIP's focus on what the project is really trying to do has allowed us not to have to make something out of nothing. It's allowed us to say what's really going on. Reporting is important, but the content of reports should reflect the content of the program, not vice versa."

• *Credibility is critical.*
Another element vital to the effectiveness of JSD would seem to be the local reputation of the national partner. The warm reception extended to JSD in Nepal owed much to the fund of good will the Budhathokis brought with them, because both had been involved in the democracy movement and, as Shobhakar remarked, "are seen as motivated not by the specific project but by the cause." "I don't know USIP, but I know Shobhakar," Pyakurel explained. "People didn't know what USIP is, but people knew who Shobhakar is. He is Nepali, he lives here, he has fought for human rights, he has worked with many people—that is how his credibility is linked with USIP's credibility, and how his credibility has enhanced USIP's."

When the international and national partner sought out local partners, their criteria prioritized organizations that reflect Nepal's remarkable diversity, are strongly rooted in their communities, and are regarded as trustworthy and credible by local people. Many of the organizations that satisfied these criteria, however, did not have the administrative and management skills needed to oversee JSD activities in their areas. The international and national partners were thus obliged to help build the organizations' capacity. This task had been foreseen but the time and effort it would require had not been planned for. Even so, the investment paid off, because by equipping locally credible organizations with the skills to sustain JSD locally, the international and national partners helped leave a legacy.

• *Interact continuously with partners and stakeholders.*
Information sharing between the international, national, and local parties and continual consultation between the partners and a wide variety of stakeholders is a labor-intensive and time-consuming task. But it is essential if that process is to become sustainable.

At the international level, staff members at USIP have consulted regularly with the U.S. State Department and INL. Such consultations help avoid or smooth over any misunderstandings or differing expectations. In the case of INL, for example, the interagency agreement between USIP and INL required a different format in order to comply with USIP's congressional mandate and ensure USIP's independence, while at the same time meeting INL's own fiscal and programmatic obligations.

USIP staff members have also reached out to a wider community of government officials, elected representatives, diplomats, scholars, NGOs, and media through a series of workshops and public events about Nepal. USIP has funded the Washington Nepal Forum, a Nepalese diaspora organization that has issued many statements directed to the Nepalese government about implementing the peace process.

The JSD national partner has also consulted regularly with a variety of international players, including the U.S. embassy, the U.S. Department of Justice's International Criminal Investigative Training Assistance Program, and representatives of other U.S. government agencies in Kathmandu, as well as many international NGOs and intergovernmental organizations active in Nepal. JSD has sought to recognize and seize opportunities for closer constructive cooperation, but it has also tried to identify potential risks of closer interaction and deliberately distanced itself from some actors at times.

At the national level, both the international and the national JSD partners have sought to maintain regular contact and good relations with the government of Nepal, briefing the ministries responsible for security and justice on forthcoming JSD activities, and meeting with the leadership of the NP and other security forces to discuss common concerns.

At the local level, the national and local partners invest a considerable amount of time in talking to the NP, political parties, local government, the judiciary, NGOs, civil society, and the community as a whole. The selection of local partners is itself a time-consuming task for the national

partner, which must identify candidates that have the appropriate experience (in areas related to security and justice) contacts (with a wide range of
stakeholders in the local community), and reputation (for fairness, honesty,
and efficiency). Once selected, however, the new local partners can play
active roles in JSD activities and lighten the burden of consultation on
the national partner. "Burden," however, is perhaps the wrong term, for
conversation with local actors is not the price JSD must pay for operating
but its very raison d'être.

• *Do not overestimate the capacity or support of stakeholders.*
The JSD partners overestimated the level of knowledge and appetite for
reform among Nepal's prosecutors, which made it impossible to carry out
police-prosecutor interactions as planned and meant that goals had to be
scaled back and refocused.

JSD has also been negatively affected by the limited support among some
political actors. Although many political leaders have publicly endorsed JSD,
some have limited understanding of the rule of law and the role of law enforcement agencies. Others, accustomed to Nepal's security forces being an
instrument of the government, seek to retain or to acquire the power to control and dictate to law enforcement agencies, and thus have resisted efforts
to promote the independence and professionalization of law enforcement
agencies, particularly the NP. Even political actors who do understand—in-
tellectually—the need for an independent police force are often constrained,
psychologically, by the zero-sum mindset that pervades much of political
life. This resistance at the policymaking level makes it all the more important
for JSD to create sustainable processes at the middle and local levels.

• *Acknowledge political sensitivities while maintaining political independence.*
At both the international and national levels, the JSD partners have discovered the need to tread carefully on politically sensitive ground, but not to
pretend that political differences do not exist. The partners have sought to
reassure stakeholders that they will not be politically embarrassed by their
participation in JSD. At the same time, however, JSD has strongly defended
its political independence.

Early on, for instance, the Maoists were suspicious of its "real" intentions
because it had been initiated by the *United States* Institute of Peace. The U.S.
embassy, for its part, was cautious because JSD sought to encourage the Maoists, whom the U.S. government had long classified as terrorists, to participate

in JSD activities. The embassy needed to ensure that USIP engaged with the Maoists independently, because the embassy had restrictions to observe. At that time, it was critical for all involved that JSD not only be an independent actor but also be seen as one. Two years later, in 2008, when the U.S. government decided to work with the Maoists to promote a stable, democratic Nepal,[19] JSD had already demonstrated to all sides that it had no hidden agenda. Since then, support from the U.S. ambassador has been consistent.

Contact between JSD partners and the government of Nepal extends beyond consultation to involve cooperation and coordination in certain areas, but JSD partners also recognize the importance of remaining, and of being seen to remain, independent of government. The politicization of security issues within Nepal makes it vital for JSD to keep in contact with the three major political parties and the seven smaller parties, any of which might react negatively to JSD activities unless kept informed in advance. Because of this scrupulous attention to relationship building, the leaders of all parties are usually ready to meet with JSD representatives at short notice.

* *Do not underestimate the time that facilitated dialogue takes.*
All the partners in Nepal underestimated the time required to get things done. Delays were not occasional problems but a constant challenge, and the sources of delay were ubiquitous:

- *Organizational.* A partnership structure demands considerable time to be spent on sharing ideas and information and coordinating efforts. Equally, a commitment to consultation with all stakeholders calls for massive investments of time and effort.
- *Logistical.* When the national partner faces power outages of up to sixteen hours per day, which has been common in Kathmandu in recent years, schedules will suffer. Provision of a generator can partly mitigate such problems, but the funds must be found to purchase, maintain, and run a generator.
- *Meteorological.* Bad weather can make it difficult or impossible to travel. In spring and the monsoon season, floods cut off parts of Nepal; during the frigid winter months, internal flights are limited.

---

19. For this shift in U.S. approach, see, for instance, "Changing U.S. Terror Policy in Nepal," *CNN World,* May 29, 2008, http://articles.cnn.com/2008-05-29/worldus.maoists_1_maoist-rebels-nepal-king-gyanendra?_s=PM:WORLD.

- *Geographic.* Getting outside Kathmandu to remote areas was key to understanding the breadth of opinion and the differing security challenges in such a diverse country. But some sites could be reached only on foot, and walking in and out of such villages could take days. The JSD team planned for some extra time for this, but the time actually required was always longer than had been anticipated.
- *Political. Bandhs* and *chakkajams* have become common ways for political actors and other organized groups to express dissatisfaction with the government. They severely disrupt the movement of people within cities and sometimes between cities, which inevitably affects travel by JSD representatives and participants. The frequent changeovers in governments and senior officials do not pose the same physical barriers to movement but do retard progress, given the need for JSD partners to form new relationships.
- *Educational.* The amount of time required to educate stakeholders about the basic concept of the rule of law and access to justice took longer than anticipated.
- *Cultural.* Personal relationships make it much easier to accomplish most things in Nepal, including securing political or bureaucratic support. But those relationships must be carefully nurtured, which demands considerable time. Schedules must also factor in Nepal's numerous religious holidays, during which the pace of business and political life slows appreciably.

- *Culture matters.*

JSD's commitment to consultation demands not only considerable time but also cultural sensitivity to the rhythm of time in Nepal. "Many foreign NGOs and the donors that fund them want to see continuous progress, but they don't understand how things really get done here," Shobhakar Budhathoki explained. "Our national focal group might meet every week, but then not for a month. A month-long religious festival means that even if you organized an event, no one would come. A visit to the NP headquarters might be no more than a cup of tea, but it might be a long discussion with the leadership. And the prep work we do might be considered a waste of time in Europe or the United States, but here it is not only a pleasure but also part of the job. We are always inviting people to our house for dinner with their wives and children, not to talk about the program, but to build relationships. Cultural awareness is vital." When Rausch visits

Nepal, she often travels with her husband and son, and all three are invariably invited to the homes of their Nepali colleagues and hosts. Similarly, when members of the national focal group visit Washington, they always have dinner at the Rausch's home. Emails always begin by asking about each other's family.

- *Personalities matter.*
The interplay of personalities has been critical to the progress made in Nepal. The willingness to embrace a new initiative, the humility to admit to past failings, the readiness to move beyond old enmities, the modesty to let others take the credit for success: these qualities are not always evident among senior members of the security forces or prominent figures in the human rights community in any country. It remains to be seen, however, whether JSD in Nepal was just lucky, or whether post-conflict circumstances and the program encourage and reward the display of such qualities.

———

These lessons are being applied not only in Nepal but also in a number of other countries emerging from conflict—such as Sudan, Iraq, and Afghanistan, where customized versions of the JSD framework are being developed.

As these and other programs evolve, a clearer idea will emerge of what conditions favor or preclude the effectiveness of the JSD approach. Experience will also help refine the lessons learned so far in Nepal about the kinds of expectations, approaches, and tactics that enhance or impede the impact of JSD. In addition, as more practitioners of facilitated dialogue acquire familiarity with JSD, they will help identify what it can offer to other forms of dialogue and what it can learn from them. Many lessons will necessarily be local in nature and applicability, and will reinforce the emphasis on customizing JSD to suit each environment in which it is adopted. But other lessons will surely have a broader applicability, for the essence of JSD—process, pragmatism, and partnership—responds to universal needs, values, and aspirations.

Appendix: Distilling the Essence of JSD

The interest in JSD has encouraged USIP to distill the essence of the program. This appendix identifies its underlying approach and key practices and includes a framework for action that could be applied in other countries emerging from conflict. A more detailed description of the JSD framework is available on request from the Rule of Law program at the United States Institute of Peace. Adapting the JSD framework to local conditions is not merely advisable but essential. JSD demands customization because it rests on the assumption that every problem requires its own solution. No single actor has all the answers: hence the need for partnerships. No magic formula lies waiting to be discovered: resolving a local problem can happen only when local actors work together and decide how to move ahead. Pragmatic concerns must be addressed with practicable solutions.

The JSD framework is thus designed to be flexible—but not infinitely elastic. Its defining characteristics can be accommodated within a variety of programmatic shapes, but each program must display features such as maximum local control, diverse participation, and a vision of justice and security as two sides of the same coin. Similarly, the sequence of steps taken by a JSD program can and will vary, but the overall direction of a program must be toward building partnerships, forging closer links between local stakeholders, and developing local capacity.

Defining Characteristics

- *Limited international management.* An international actor (or actors) helps launch the JSD process and shepherds it, at least through its early stages, but international involvement is deliberately limited and focused on facilitation and provision of technical advice rather than direction.
- *Maximum local ownership.* The spectrum of local involvement extends from input to participation, cooperation, management, ownership, and control; constant efforts are made to maximize local involvement and ownership.
- *Stakeholder readiness for dialogue.* JSD is launched only when one or more stakeholders has shown an interest in building understanding or even cooperating with other stakeholders at local and national levels.
- *Partnership mode.* The international actor (the international partner) forms a partnership (not donor-recipient or vendor-client relationships) with a national-level actor (the national partner) to develop and implement JSD programs; the national partner forms partnerships with local actors (the local partners) and coordinates and monitors local JSD activities while feeding information back to the international partner.

- *Good reputation and access of partners.* All partners are and are seen to be credible, committed, trustworthy, and independent; each has access to leading figures and officials at its level; partners must be seen as either politically neutral individually or as politically balanced collectively.
- *Local focus informed by general principles.* JSD introduces stakeholders to general rule of law principles and typical post-conflict reconstruction roles, but dialogues focus on local issues and perspectives.
- *Diversity of participation.* JSD brings together groups that tend not to work closely together; the participants representing those groups are also varied (in rank, profession, area of interest, political affiliation, geographic location, gender, ethnicity, and so on); the staff of the national and local partners are also diverse in terms of gender, ethnicity, and so on.
- *Equal respect for the interests, values, and agendas of all stakeholders.* The concerns and ambitions of the police are treated as no less important than those of civil society; all active local political parties are afforded equal opportunities to hear and be heard; cultural awareness and sensitivity are vital.
- *Justice and security seen as mutually supportive.* Security and justice are seen as two sides of the same coin; security is interpreted broadly to mean a society that not only maintains civil order and enforces laws but also respects human rights and reflects social diversity; justice is understood to mean not only an independent judiciary and due process of law but also popular conceptions of fairness, equality of treatment, and accountability.
- *Long-term perspective.* By necessity or design, JSD takes a long view: partnerships take time to form; initial dialogues last only a few days but are intended to kick-start an enduring process of regular consultation and cooperation between local actors; immediate concrete results are welcome but not expected; some initiatives may bear fruit quickly, but there is no less merit in planting seeds that will not germinate for a long time; local-level ideas and achievements percolate slowly upward into national-level policymaking; much of the focus is on establishing relationships and structures that will naturally sustain themselves once the international partner departs.
- *Consultation and sharing of information.* The partners consult constantly with one another and regularly with all stakeholders at all levels; information is shared on an ongoing basis except where confidentiality, safety, or program effectiveness dictate otherwise.

- *Maintenance of close contact and good relations with government.* Contact with the national government extends beyond consultation to involve cooperation and coordination in some areas, but the JSD process must remain independent from government.
- *Ongoing evaluation of activities.* Assessment of major initiatives as well as ongoing programs is crucial, with steps taken being chronicled, reasons for success or failure analyzed, and lessons drawn and woven into future plans.
- *Calibrated public outreach and profile.* JSD initiatives are publicized in advance and their results disseminated in print or online reports, but the media are kept at a distance early in the process and invited to cover later activities on a case-by-case basis; JSD program's public profile is usually kept low and continually monitored and adjusted in light of current initiatives, changes in political conditions, and shifts in the agendas of stakeholders.

JSD in Action

JSD programs will follow different evolutionary paths, but most are likely to feature many of the activities undertaken by JSD in Nepal. The sequence of those activities in Nepal follows, but many activities were iterative or are ongoing. An apt metaphor for JSD in Nepal is of a river rather than a ladder.

1. Recognize the need for JSD by conducting an assessment of local needs or requesting local actors for assistance.
2. Identify credible national partner with national-level access.
3. Make contact with national-level stakeholders in government, security agencies and forces, civil society, political parties, and so on.
4. Demonstrate bona fides, such as evidence of relevant expertise, track records in comparable situations, development of useful materials.
5. Launch initial, broad-ranging discussion of security situation and rule of law principles between national-level stakeholders.
6. Conduct series of facilitated dialogues in capital city or other city with close ties to policymaking community.
7. Develop local contacts and partnerships who can help organize community-level dialogues and identify participants.
8. Ensure that local partners have capacity to undertake dialogues, and provide training or resources where necessary.

9. Conduct a series of facilitated dialogues between local actors (such as police and civil society) in various locations throughout the country, to last at least two days and follow the same format:

- Day 1. In the first half of the day, police participants discuss the challenges confronting them and possible solutions; in the other half, civil society participants do the same; both sessions begin with the international or national partner exploring definitions of key concepts, challenges, and roles and past international experiences.
- Day 2, session 1. Police and civil society present their thoughts to one another, discuss them, and jointly devise possible solutions.
- Day 2, session 2. Police and civil society representatives present their joint concerns and solutions to representatives of local political parties, who then discuss among themselves what they have heard.

10. Sustain and build on local momentum by instituting regular and local meetings; securing action to address concerns identified at the dialogue, responding to local concerns and issues as they arise.

11. Assess results of local-level dialogues and options for additional programming.

12. Create high-level national focal group to help shape JSD strategy, make key tactical decisions, keep high-level government officials informed of progress, and the like.

13. Develop strategy for future programming based on assessment of recent dialogues and with input from focal group.

14. Create physical infrastructure such as permanent venue for police–civil society interaction and national program office with workspace and meeting space.

15. Encourage closer cooperation among justice- and security-sector actors, such as police and prosecutors' offices.

16. Develop parallel and complementary activities, such as a national survey of concerns about and hopes for the justice and security system.

17. Expand the security and justice dialogues to many more districts and to cover additional topics of concern.

18. Provide tools and skills training to develop the administrative and organizational capacity of local partners and thereby enable them to develop and conduct effective programming by themselves.

19. Support efforts by the police to institutionalize public engagement.
20. Generate discussion on local implementation of national policy-level strategies for improving police-community relations.
21. Evaluate the impact of JSD programming, comparing program evolution with public perceptions and crime rates.
22. Gradually reduce international support as JSD becomes fully locally sustainable.

Conclusion

Daniel Serwer and David R. Smock

T he case studies in this volume cover a wide variety of conflict situations and peacemaking efforts, but some lessons from experiences apply generally.

Facilitators

The role of the facilitator is critical. It would be counterproductive for a facilitator to approach a facilitated dialogue with the assumption of being simply a neutral traffic cop. A skilled facilitator needs to be actively engaged in directing the discussion and helping the participants reach consensus. The facilitator needs to have become an expert on the conflict and on devising possible ways forward. As the Kosovo case illustrates, full engagement by the facilitator demands a great deal of sustained intellectual effort and physical and emotional stamina. This experience was replicated in Nepal and the other cases in this volume.

In all these cases, the impartiality of the facilitators was critical to the success of the peacebuilding processes. In the Nepal case, for example, USIP needed initially to ensure that it was perceived as independent of the U.S. embassy, which still had restrictions on dealing with the Maoists, who were suspicious of any U.S. involvement. Local partners likewise needed to establish that they were willing and able to consult broadly and impartially. Both the foreign and local facilitators had to be perceived by all participants as impartial and prepared to conduct an open process incorporating all stakeholders.

Local facilitators play a central role. In Diyala and Mahmoudiya, the peacebuilding processes were constructed around the Iraqi facilitators. USIP staff involved credited them with much of the success of the projects. In both cases, the Iraqi facilitators had been selected and trained by USIP before these two projects were initiated. In the Niger Delta, the project organizer went to considerable lengths to select and prepare the six Nigerian facilitators, who were called mediators. Two were selected from each of the three ethnic groups in conflict on the basis of their reputations within the communities and their breadth of perspective. As chapter 7 makes clear, "The long-term solution is to empower local actors with the technical knowledge, hands-on experience, and confidence that will enable them to gradually assume full control of the dialogue process."

Synthesizing the roles of foreign and local facilitators is also important. Some of these cases, such as Mahmoudiya and Diyala, illustrate the possibility of foreign and local facilitators working in harmony with one another. In others, such as the Colombia civil society case, the local partners take the lead role. In still others, such as Kosovo, foreign facilitators dominated and their dominant roles were accepted. However, in the Alexandria process, resentment grew—particularly among the Christian participants—toward the foreign facilitator, who was also a Christian. Given the sharp divisions among the three religious communities, it would have been difficult to identify a local facilitator who would have been acceptable to all three communities. It may thus have been necessary to have a foreign facilitator, but his role was nevertheless resented.

Collaborating with local partner organizations is ideal. In both of the cases from Colombia, USIP worked effectively with existing Colombian organizations. Catholic and evangelical organizations were brought together through USIP's intervention. The projects could not have advanced as far as they did without them as collaborators. In fact, in the Colombian civil society organizations, the USIP facilitator almost invariably bowed to the guidance given by the partner organizations. In the Alexandria process, a new local organization was created under the project umbrella. The Alexandria process itself became an organization, although a struggling one. The offshoots of the Alexandria process, namely, Mosaica and the Council of Religious Institutions of the Holy Land, were built on stronger institutional bases and have outlived the Alexandria process. Something similar happened in Kosovo, where a "Council of Professionals" grew out of the USIP dialogue and continued for years thereafter to play an important role in interethnic dialogue in the Gjilan/Gnjilane community.

Timing and Planning

The importance of timing cannot be overstated. All the projects described in this volume struggled with the issue of whether their initiative was coming at a ripe moment. Some experienced false starts because they discovered that it was not the right moment to proceed. The Nepal case devotes significant attention in the write-up to the assessment of whether that situation was ripe for intervention.

Civil society has considerable peacebuilding potential. Recognizing this and tapping it is indispensable. All the projects described in this volume were built on the premise that civil society organizations and leaders can play valuable roles in peacebuilding. It is not necessary, or even in many cases prudent, to wait for Track I processes to take the lead. Unofficial processes rooted in civil society can, if properly guided and nurtured, push the peace-building envelope.

Initiatives with any bearing on national policies need to incorporate link-ages to Track 1 diplomacy. In both Colombian cases, the projects hoped to influence government policy in promoting peace. Similarly, the Alexandria process hoped to provide a religious peacemaking track to reinforce a secular-political process. Unfortunately, because the political process did not gain traction, the value of the religious track was limited. The Nigerian project was initiated in part because the state government failed in its effort to launch a successful peace process, but the ultimate success of the Track II process depended on reinforcement from the state government. In the Diyala case, the failure of both local officials and international agencies to recognize and build on the groundwork laid by the civil society process led to severe shortcomings in the official efforts.

Focus on the future is as important as recognizing the past. People who have suffered severely from intergroup conflict usually need to tell their stories of the atrocities they experienced before they can consider a shared future. In the Kosovo meetings, participants needed to tell their stories and be convinced that they were heard by the other side before they could talk about the future. This was also true of the Niger Delta project and the Mahmoudiya projects. In all three, the organizers established as the projects' goals the setting out of a shared vision for the future. The Kosovo and Mahmoudiya projects set out specific scenarios for the future and had the participants identify the steps they needed to take together to get there. They were able to do so only after their past suffering had been acknowledged.

Be sure to engage alternative voices, or lay the groundwork for it, from the beginning. The Colombian civil society project has encountered considerable difficulty involving groups in the project who were not present at the outset. This is explained both by the groups that have been involved from the beginning being reluctant to engage alternative voices, and by those outside the process who felt excluded from the beginning. The problem is particularly severe between moderates who are promoting peace and hardliners who oppose any accommodation or compromises. Frequently, the moderates are prepared to engage in dialogue but the militants remain outside the process.

The difficulties of working in an active conflict zone are inevitable but must be confronted pragmatically. Most of the projects related in this volume were organized in zones where violence was still active. Some participants in the Kosovo and Mahmoudiya processes were murdered. Some situations required armored vehicles to transport participants and armed guards at the dialogue site. In such circumstances, any comment a participant made might put that person in physical danger, as was true in the Niger Delta. Facilitators were often in jeopardy as well. These peacebuilding projects were not for the squeamish.

Both the Alexandria process in Israel-Palestine and the intrafaith dialogue in Colombia underscored the value of working with religious communities, but also demonstrated the difficulty of doing so. The facilitator in the civil society project in Colombia lamented the difficulty of engaging religious leaders in Colombia in that project, because they constituted an important stakeholder. Religious leaders played a critical role in the Kosovo dialogue as well, with Serb Orthodox clerics playing an important role in enlisting the participation of the Serb community more broadly while at the same time introducing problematic issues concerning the status of the church and its property.

Power imbalances need to be taken into account when planning an initiative. The religious dialogue project in Colombia illustrated the difficulties encountered when one group has much less experience and controls less power than the other. The facilitator in the Colombian project had to ensure that the more powerful community, the Catholics, were not allowed to impose their theology or to move more quickly than the Protestants. Similar problems were encountered in the interfaith dialogue project in Israel-Palestine and in the facilitation between Kosovar Serbs and Albanians. Accommodations need to be made by providing extra time or special training for the less advantaged community. The facilitator must be alert to the sensitivities the disadvantaged community might have because of its status.

That dialogue alone will not—or only rarely can—resolve a conflict must be acknowledged. Conflicts may derive from competition for, or inequitable distribution of, resources or power. These inequities need to be addressed. The Kosovo, Mahmoudiya, and Niger Delta projects focused on shared visions for the future, including steps necessary to reach that future. The best outcome from a facilitated dialogue is a joint plan of action that will guide the communities in conflict in addressing the root causes of the conflict. The Nepal project moved from improved understanding to joint proposals and finally to joint action.

Recognize that effective dialogue may require a great deal of time. This was clear in the Colombian intrafaith dialogue. The facilitator realized that a compressed process might cause one or more of the communities to resist the pace. The Nigerian dialogue continued over a decade. The Kosovo dialogue engaged several different configurations of dialogical partners over several years. In Nepal, the organizers recognized from the outset that the project would require years rather than merely weeks or months.

Process

Weigh the trade-offs between the participants representing their institutions versus participating in their personal capacities. Frequently, participants in facilitated dialogue are prepared to engage only if they can participate in their personal capacities. To serve as representatives of their institutions may burden the dialogue, the participants always having to refer to their institutions for instructions on how to proceed. And yet, a fundamental shortcoming of the Alexandria process was that the participants did not represent their communities, only themselves. The creation of the follow-on dialogue in the form of the Council of the Religious Institutions of the Holy Land came about in part to overcome this weakness. That participants represented their religious institutions provided greater continuity and less turnover, but also more constrained contributions to the dialogue.

Intragroup dynamics often need to be addressed first. In Kosovo, the project encountered severe fissures within both the Serb and Albanian communities. Separate intragroup peacebuilding efforts had to be undertaken before intergroup encounters could be organized. Once the Albanians and Serbs had met separately and laid out their own plans for achieving group goals, they were much more ready and willing to meet with their adversaries to discuss how their ethnically defined objectives might or might not find some degree of mutual accommodation. Similarly, in the ecumenical project in Colombia, it became clear that intergroup progress could be achieved only if intragroup dynamics were addressed first, that is, among Protestants and among Catholics separately before meeting together.

Recognize that some participants may want the conflict to continue. In the Niger Delta, the facilitator recognized, after watching the disruptive behavior of some participants, that they had a vested interest, particularly financial, in an ongoing conflict. Dialogue could not be successful unless it was seen as opening up the possibility of economic benefits.

Particularly in those projects that set out shared goals for the future it is important to monitor progress toward achieving those goals. The Kosovo project demonstrated the need for follow-up when the initial pledges of action failed to materialize. But it is not always easy to have independent monitors in place to assess progress being made. The Mahmoudiya project in Iraq demonstrated the value of having the local facilitators who helped manage the dialogue process remain engaged to hold the participants to the promises they made for joint action.

Documenting the dialogue and peacebuilding process is important for several reasons. Those who managed the Mahmoudiya process, for example, lamented that at least parts of the process had not been documented in a video, which could have been used as an education tool in confronting other conflicts in Iraq or elsewhere. If a video had been too intrusive into a sensitive process, at least a written document detailing the process, including both successes and obstacles encountered, could have been prepared and disseminated. Joint concluding statements from the Mahmoudiya, Diyala, and Kosovo processes were invaluable in providing benchmarks for future behavior and planning.

It is widely recognized that facilitated dialogue and Track II diplomacy usually fail to include systematic evaluation of both output and outcomes. The need for monitoring progress in implementing commitments made during the dialogue is clear. But it is also important to evaluate the dialogue process itself. Of the cases presented in this volume, only the Colombia civil society project did so systematically. By administering questionnaires after each dialogue session, the facilitator was able to make midcourse corrections to the process. Even in this case, however, the organizers measured output more than outcomes.

Summary

These dialogue efforts were undertaken in notably different contexts using approaches that were not standardized, but each in its own way illustrates the value of facilitating joint problem solving and planning at various levels when key stakeholders can be brought together around a limited set of common objectives. Even though higher-level political and military conflicts are ongoing, it is possible to engage local communities on subconflicts that would otherwise complicate the larger peacebuilding process.

All of the efforts described here were undertaken after a considerable violence, which in several instances was also ongoing. This violence enormously complicated dialogue and made it difficult for the communities involved to realistically weigh the benefits of collaboration, even if it also gave them strong incentives to make at least some progress toward reducing the risks of future violence. Whether facilitated dialogue undertaken at an earlier stage—before any significant violence took place—might have been productive is an open question. It certainly would make sense to try, though finding resources for dialogue before major violence breaks out is difficult. Nor is it easy to convince communities to take the risk of dialogue when a great deal of effort is still going into stoking the fires of conflict.

USIP's peculiar status—nongovernmental and unofficial but funded by the U.S. Congress—weighed both positively and negatively in undertaking these efforts. On the one hand, participants often felt that USIP sponsorship gave the efforts more prospects for success, and for eventual funding of initiatives growing out of the dialogues. On the other hand, association with the U.S. government could be problematic, because official Washington was rarely viewed as completely impartial or disinterested. In general, however, the facilitators were able to establish a unique identity more rooted in USIP's peacebuilding mission than in the perception of affiliation with the U.S. government or USIP's formal status as a nongovernmental organization.

People in conflict are anxious to have their concerns taken seriously, and most of them understand that they will eventually need to live with their adversaries whether they like it or not. USIP is by far not the only organization to have established bona fides with opposing sides in a violent conflict—many nongovernmental organizations and some government and intergovernmental ones are repeatedly successful at this. Each organization will bring to the task its own advantages and disadvantages. USIP's accomplishments are certainly not unique. A great deal more effort and experimentation is needed to discover more about what works and what does not in particular circumstances. But it is clear that facilitating dialogue has enormous potential to help restore relationships and give communities an alternative to violence.

About the Contributors

Judith Burdin Asuni is executive director of Academic Associates Peace-Works, a Nigerian NGO working in the fields of conflict management, peace and development, and peace education. An American by birth and Nigerian by naturalization, she has lived in Nigeria for forty years and worked in the conflict resolution field since 1992. She is best known for her work in the Niger Delta, especially with members of the armed groups. She was a Jennings Randolph Senior Fellow at USIP in 2009–10.

Rusty Barber is the former director of Iraq Programs at USIP, a position he assumed after serving as chief of party for the Institute's field mission in Iraq from 2007 to 2008. Before joining USIP, he was a member of the Foreign Service, serving in Pakistan and at the U.S. mission to the Organization for Security and Co-operation in Europe, where he focused on conflict prevention in Central Asia. From 1990 to 2001, he was president of Voyageur East, a global import and trade consulting company.

Virginia M. Bouvier is a senior program officer for the Center of Innovation at USIP and heads its Colombia conflict team. She was formerly assistant professor of Latin American literature and culture at the University of Maryland and a senior associate at the Washington Office on Latin America. She is the editor of *Colombia: Building Peace in a Time of War* and *The Globalization of U.S.-Latin American Relations: Democracy, Intervention, and Human Rights*, and author and editor of other books.

Susan Hayward has been senior program officer in the Religion and Peace-making Center at USIP since 2007. She works with religious communities in Sri Lanka, Colombia, and Iraq to strengthen their participation in peacebuilding processes. Before joining USIP, she worked with the Academy of Educational Development in Colombo, Sri Lanka, and with the Carter Center. She was formerly a fellow of the Program on Negotiation at Harvard Law School.

Lucy Kurtzer-Ellenbogen is a senior program officer at the Center for Conflict Management at USIP, where she coordinates the Institute's work on the Arab-Israeli conflict and on Egypt. Before joining USIP, she consulted on Arabic media discourse, with a special focus on language in conflict situations and the expression of identity relations. Earlier she worked with the Department of State as an Arabic language specialist and as a program officer at the Kennedy School of Government's Middle East Initiative.

Caelan McGee is a mediator and facilitator with experience in post-conflict reconstruction, as well as land use and natural resource disputes. A senior program officer at USIP, he spent two years in USIP's Baghdad office working with provincial government and training Iraqis in facilitation and mediation. Before joining USIP, he helped design and facilitate multistakeholder processes to resolve conflicts related to transportation planning and environmental disturbance in the United States, Mexico, and Papua New Guinea.

Nigel Quinney is president of The Editorial Group and has worked in the field of conflict resolution for twenty years, as an editor, writer, and researcher. His long association with USIP includes projects to promote security and justice in post-conflict societies. He is co-author of *American Negotiating Behavior* and *Negotiating with Groups That Use Terror*. He is also a consultant to European and American think tanks, educational institutions, publishers, and corporations, and adjunct faculty at the California State University–San Marcos.

Colette Rausch is director of USIP's Rule of Law Center of Innovation. Her focus is on criminal justice and police reform initiatives, which have included projects in Afghanistan, Guatemala, Kosovo, Liberia, Nicaragua, Peru, and Nepal. Before joining the Institute, she worked at the Organization for Security and Co-operation in Europe mission in Kosovo. Previously, she was with the U.S. Department of Justice, as resident legal adviser in Hungary and later in Bosnia, and as program manager for Central and East Europe, establishing criminal justice development and training projects in Albania, Bosnia, Croatia, Kosovo, and Macedonia.

Daniel Serwer is professor of conflict management at the Johns Hopkins School of Advanced International Studies and a scholar at the Middle East Institute. He has also taught at George Washington and Georgetown universities. He was formerly vice president of the Centers of Peacebuilding Innovation at USIP, where he led teams on law, religion, economics, media, technology, security sector governance, and gender. He also served as vice president for USIP's Peace and Stability Operations. He came to USIP as a senior fellow on Balkan regional security in 1998. Before that, he was a minister-counselor at the U.S. Department of State, where he won six performance awards. He served from 1994 to 1996 as U.S. special enjoy and coordinator for the Bosnian Federation, mediating between Croats and Muslims and negotiating the first agreement reached at the Dayton peace talks.

David R. Smock is senior vice president at USIP and director of the Religion and Peacemaking Center. Previously he directed the Institute's grant program. He has held executive-level positions at International Voluntary Services, the United Church of Christ, the Institute of International Education, and the Ford Foundation, where he served in Kenya, Nigeria, Ghana, Lebanon, and New York. He is the author or editor of eleven books, including *Interfaith Dialogue and Peacebuilding* and *The Politics of Pluralism*.

George Ward is based at the Institute for Defense Analysis. He was previously senior vice president for International Programs at World Vision. From 1999 to 2005, he was vice president and director of the Professional Training Program at USIP. In 2003, he served as U.S. coordinator for humanitarian assistance in Iraq. Ward was a Foreign Service officer for thirty years. As ambassador to Namibia, he managed a successful humanitarian de-mining program and a campaign against gender violence. From 1992 to 1996, he was principal deputy assistant secretary of state, with responsibilities for U.S. policy on the United Nations and other international organizations.

About the
United States Institute of Peace

The United States Institute of Peace is an independent, nonpartisan institution established and funded by Congress. The Institute provides analysis, training, and tools to help prevent, manage, and end violent international conflicts, promote stability, and professionalize the field of peacebuilding.